Twillingate

Family Stories of Adventure and Loss

PRISCILLA JAYNE DENEHY

Twillingate – Family Stories of Adventure and Loss

First Edition, 2019
ISBN 978-1-09045-148-4 (paperback)

Independently Published

Printed in the United States of America

In memory of

My grandparents
James & Elizabeth Primmer
and their children
Lucy, Heber, Susannah, Gladys, and Hilda

&

My parents
Gordon & Gladys Harnum
and their eldest children
Neil James, Uldine Cavell, Edna Louise, and Gordon Lester

FOREWORD

by Brian Gordon Walker

"You were in first grade?" asked Heber.

I asked that question while interviewing my grandfather in 1977. Priscilla has woven it into the storyline with many other quotes from those tapes and so many family stories - a lifetime of stories - the life of Gladys Curtis Harnum (*nee* Primmer).

This is a book about the Primmer and Harnum families as we migrated from Newfoundland to live in the eastern United States during the 20th Century. Priscilla presents it through her mother's narrative and with stories from her father Gordon and her sisters. They are stories that Priscilla has heard and lived. They are stories that she wants us to know.

Gladys was a wonderful matriarch with a keen sense of humor, an intense love for her family, and a willingness "to speak the truth" about people as she saw them. In these stories she tells us that some have imperfections and some have real flaws. Are there stories that are not being told?

Twillingate - Family Stories of Adventure and Loss is a clear chronicle of events during her lifetime, but even after her death more than twenty years ago, we feel that Gladys is speaking to us, that she is ready to answer our questions, to tell us more. She sheds new perspective on events that we experienced and details those that happened before we were born or in which we were not involved.

When Gordon and Gladys were alive, Gordon won praise for his storytelling. Gladys finally gets to tell her stories!

PREFACE & ACKNOWLEDGMENTS

I am indebted to my extended family in the United States and Newfoundland for providing many stories and valuable family information.

I am also blessed to have had such wonderful parents, Gordon Hedley Harnum and Gladys Curtis Primmer Harnum, the main characters of *Twillingate*.

To my nephew, Brian Walker, a multitude of thanks for your encouragement and support and for having the foresight to record my father's life story in his own voice before the end of his life.

To my friend, Denise Parmentier, who transcribed Brian's recordings and spent hours editing, re-writing, and researching information for *Twillingate*. She added needed color to my plain Newfoundland sentences, and most of all encouraged me to finish my story.

Thanks also to my cousin, Elizabeth Troake, for providing answers to my many questions and clarification of past events in Newfoundland.

Priscilla Jayne Denehy

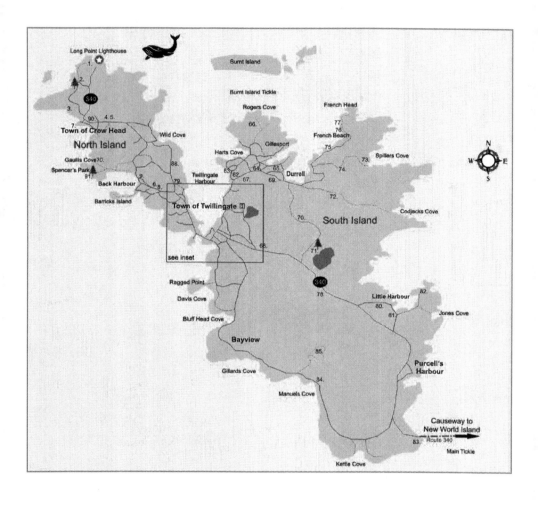

Town of Twillingate
The Primmer family lived in Harts Cove.
map used with permission

CONTENTS

FOREWORD iv

PREFACE & ACKNOWLEDGMENTS v

THE BEOTHUK. xi

CAST OF CHARACTERS xiv

GORDON – THE LIE. 1

1920s

Chapter 1 - THE JOURNEY 4

Chapter 2 - ISLAND LIFE 7

Chapter 3 - DAILY CHORES. 9

Chapter 4 - ISLAND LIFE CONTINUED 11

Chapter 5 - STORYTELLING 13

Chapter 6 - ENTER GORDON. 16

Chapter 7 - HEART'S DELIGHT 21

Chapter 8 - NORTH STATION, BOSTON 22

Chapter 9 - A VISIT FROM GORDON HARNUM. 23

Chapter 10 - NEW YORK 28

Chapter 11 - RETURN TO BOSTON 31

Chapter 12 - THE WEDDING 33

Chapter 13 - HARD TIMES AHEAD. 39

Chapter 14 - AN UNEXPECTED SURPRISE. 42

Chapter 15 - GORDON SPEAKS 43

Chapter 16 - FAMILY MATTERS 46

Chapter 17 - THE GREAT DEPRESSION 48

Chapter 18 - THERE IS ALWAYS HOPE 49

Chapter 19 - NEIL JAMES HARNUM 50

Chapter 20 - SUICIDE OFF THE CHARLES RIVER BRIDGE 52

1930s

Chapter 21 - HOMEWARD BOUND. 56

Chapter 22 - RETURN TO TWILLINGATE 57

Chapter 23 - **A VISIT TO EVA** 59

Chapter 24 - **MY RETURN** 62

Chapter 25 - **HOME AT LAST** 64

Chapter 26 - **GORDON TALKS** 66

Chapter 27 - **EXPLOSION!** 68

Chapter 28 - **BY THE SEAT OF HIS PANTS** 69

Chapter 29 - **LOCKE STREET** 71

Chapter 30 - **CHRISTMAS EVE** 73

Chapter 31 - **DIAMOND REO** 75

Chapter 32 - **A VISIT FROM COUSIN WILF** 80

Chapter 33 - **RIGGING SCHOOL AT THE GREEN PARROT** 82

Chapter 34 - **EIGHT CHETWYND ROAD** 84

1940s

Chapter 35 - **RATIONING** 88

Chapter 36 - **ALL IN THE FAMILY** 89

Chapter 37 - **WORLD WAR II** 90

Chapter 38 - **THE HUMAN FLY** 93

Chapter 39 - **NEW YORK CITY** 95

Chapter 40 - **CAMBRIDGE** 97

Chapter 41 - **"THE SHOP"** 98

Chapter 42 - **ROMANCE IS IN THE AIR** 99

Chapter 43 - **JIM TAKES A JOYRIDE** 101

Chapter 44 - **FAREWELL TO LUCY** 105

Chapter 45 - **TWILLINGATE REVISITED** 108

Chapter 46 - **PRISCILLA JAYNE HARNUM** 111

Chapter 47 - **THE BOYS** 113

Chapter 48 - **THE GIRLS** 115

1950s

Chapter 49 - **TRAIN TO AMARILLO** 120

Chapter 50 - **ENTER EARL** 124

Chapter 51 - **FAREWELL TO FATHER** 125

Chapter 52 - **THE CAPE – MARION** 125

Chapter 53 - **MARION, MASSACHUSETTS** 127

Chapter 54 - DEXTER BEACH 129

Chapter 55 - HURRICANE CAROL 130

Chapter 56 - BILL JOINS UP 134

Chapter 57 - NEW ADDITIONS 136

Chapter 58 - THE COTTAGE 138

Chapter 59 - SHERMAN STREET 143

Chapter 60 - YOUNG GORDON 145

Chapter 61 - FAREWELL TO FRANK 148

Chapter 62 - PONY AND PUPPY RACES 149

Chapter 63 - THE TOTEM POLE BALLROOM 151

Chapter 64 - THE MOVIE CAMERA 153

Chapter 65 - PRISCILLA'S NEWFOUNDLAND TRIP 156

Chapter 66 - ST. JOHN'S TO TWILLINGATE 158

Chapter 67 - FRANNIE & BILL 162

1960s

Chapter 68 - GRANDCHILDREN 166

Chapter 69 - THE MOVE TO BELMONT 167

Chapter 70 - RESETTLEMENT 171

Chapter 71 - SANDWICH 173

Chapter 72 - HOWIE 175

Chapter 73 - BELMONT HIGH 176

Chapter 74 - THE GAS EXPLOSION 177

Chapter 75 - EARL GOES TO BELCHERTOWN 178

Chapter 76 - NEWFOUNDLAND BY VW BUS 180

Chapter 77 - UNA MISIÓN A MÉXICO & THE STETSON HAT 182

Chapter 78 - CONFESSIONAL 184

Chapter 79 - KIMBERLY LOUISE FAIR 187

Chapter 80 - THERE'S SOMETHING ABOUT MARY 188

Chapter 81 - SOLD! 191

Chapter 82 - A TRIP TO NEWFOUNDLAND 192

Chapter 83 - GONE! 194

Chapter 84 - KIDNEY SURGERY 196

Chapter 85 - LAKEWORTH, FLORIDA 197

1970s

Chapter 86 - DEANNA DOROTHEA 200

Chapter 87 - LARRY'S TRAGIC DEATH 202

Chapter 88 - RETURNING HOME WITHOUT LARRY 205

Chapter 89 - HEBER 207

Chapter 90 - STEVEN 209

Chapter 91 - ALL MY GRANDCHILDREN 211

Chapter 92 - MINK JACKET 213

Chapter 93 - 50th WEDDING ANNIVERSARY 215

1980s

Chapter 94 - DANNY & GARY 218

Chapter 95 - ARIZONA OR BUST! (PRISCILLA RETURNS) 221

Chapter 96 - LAST TRIP TO NEWFOUNDLAND 226

Chapter 97 - THE RIDE HOME 232

Chapter 98 - DOT DRIVES BACK 233

Chapter 99 - DOT MOVES TO FLORIDA 235

Chapter 100 - UNCLE BILL HARNUM 237

Chapter 101 - GORDON HEDLEY HARNUM 239

Chapter 102 - FAREWELL TO GORDON (ENTER ANNA) 241

Chapter 103 - ST. JAMES'S CHURCH, CAMBRIDGE 243

Chapter 104 - THE PEACE CORPS 245

Chapter 105 - TRIP TO NEWFOUNDLAND 1989 248

Chapter 106 - PRISCILLA & ED 251

1990s

Chapter 107 - TRIP TO NEWFOUNDLAND 1991 254

Chapter 108 - TRIP TO NEWFOUNDLAND 1992 256

Chapter 109 - 85TH BIRTHDAY 258

Chapter 110 - GLADYS'S FAREWELL 261

RECIPES 263

G. H. HARNUM, INC 264

THE MEMORY WALL 265

THE BEOTHUK

The story of the Beothuk is fascinating and controversial . . . it is generally believed that they are distant relatives of the Algonquin. They came to Newfoundland from Labrador across the 18 kilometer wide Strait of Belle Isle. Beothuk living sites and burial grounds abound in Newfoundland. It is believed that they inhabited the land for almost 2,000 years.

(https://www.mysteriesofcanada.com/newfoundland/beothuk)

A young Indian woman named **Shanawdithit** (spellings vary) is generally considered the last living member of the Beothuk tribe, although there are people today who claim ancestry. Starving and alone, she and her mother and sister were taken by the British. Shanawdithit lived for six years as a servant known as "Nancy," drawing pictures and telling stories of her lost tribe. She died of tuberculosis in 1829.

According to some accounts Shanawdithit's aunt Demasduit had just given birth when the British raided her village. Her husband, the Red Indian Lake chief, was killed trying to protect her. Her baby was left behind, and by the time she learned enough English to explain this to the British, the infant had starved to death. Demasduit also died from tuberculosis.

(https://www.bigorrin.org/beothuk_kids.htm)

It was the Beothuk culture to distrust people outside of their tribe and members who associated with others were not allowed back into the tribe. Because of their isolation, they were easily driven inland from the Newfoundland coast, away from their source of food, and starvation was the cause of many deaths.

Near Twillingate by Aidan Haley

courtesy of aidanhaleyart.com, used with permission

Map of Newfoundland and Labrador

courtesy of Natural Resources Canada, used with permission

CAST OF CHARACTERS

Gladys Primmer – A plain and innocent young girl, straight off the boat from Newfoundland. There was more to Gladys than met the eye.

Elizabeth (Smith) Primmer – Gladys's mother. Rumored to be descended from the aboriginal Beothuk tribe. A warm-hearted, kind soul, she poured tea over troubled waters to keep her family united.

James Primmer – Gladys's father. A fisherman and native Newfoundlander. Stern, authoritarian, he ran his outport saltbox house like he was commanding a ship.

Heber Primmer – Gladys's only brother, stricken with polio as a youth. He managed to get around just fine, but a cherubic face and manner belied Heber's love for playing pranks.

Hilda Primmer – Youngest of the Primmer clan. A solemn child, she didn't say much, but she was eager to have her parents all to herself.

Paddy – A St. Bernard/Newfoundland cross. The beloved family pet, all he was missing was a wooden keg of brandy attached to his collar.

Grandfather Primmer – An Englishman, complete with red hair and a tall, sturdy physique, he had a very Irish look. Gone but not forgotten, his strong back and arms yielded a legacy of rich fertile soil that kept his family rolling in potatoes.

Puss – A cat with more than nine lives. Her fondness for licking cream got her into deep trouble.

Susannah (Sue or Sally) Primmer – Gladys's older sister. She braved the icy cold waters off the coast of Twillingate for a share of booty from wreckage of ships that struck the icebergs. Married to Frank they lived a respectable life in Boston.

Gordon Harnum – Blue-eyed golden boy. He said he was a liar, but Gladys couldn't keep her eyes off him. He was orphaned at eight and raised by his sister. Gordon was charming, and usually got what he wanted.

Lucy (Luce) Primmer – The oldest of Gladys's sisters. Luce was a hardworking nurse at Mercy Hospital. She married Steve Sweetapple, a carpenter and hard New Yorker. He had the tools and the skill, but he was fonder of drink than work.

James Harnum and **Sarah Wiseman** – Gordon's long gone parents. They had an arranged marriage that villagers whispered was a 'fishy' business.

GORDON – THE LIE

My first childhood memory was when I was six. I lied to my mother and she put me into the dark closet under the stairs. I wasn't afraid of the dark or the lack of space, barely enough for a boy sidled up against a flour barrel. It was the feeling of being trapped in there that scared me. Trapped like a rabbit in a box. It seemed like forever before my mother came to let me out.

"Now have ye' learned a lesson then?" She hauled me up by my arm and lectured me about liars. "Their good excuses are nothin'. If yer always tellin' lies none will believe ye' when there's truth to tell." I can't recall the lie, but the closet under the stairs, now, that I can remember . . . like it was yesterday.

From that day till my last on Earth, I had no use for liars.

Portrait (clockwise from left), James, Eva, Sarah, Gordon, and William (Jordan) Harnum circa 1909

1920s

CHAPTER 1

THE JOURNEY

February 1927
GLADYS

I clung to my mother and struggled with the thought that I might never see her again. Maybe I should stay.

"Your brother and sisters will be there for you," she said in her crisp island accent. "You'll be in my prayers, Gladys, and you will do just fine. You're smart and hardworking, you'll have no trouble finding work there." With tears running down my cheeks, she hugged me once more. Her arms warmed around me, keeping out the cold and unknown.

Father reached out, embraced me briefly, and kissed my cheek. "You'll do fine girl, come back when you can." He quickly turned away.

My father is "Master" of the house, strict and sometimes overbearing. No one dared cross him. His name is James Primmer, but most folks in Twillingate called him Jimmy. Mother was born just plain Elizabeth Smith.

I would miss all of them. I was leaving for America today. My sister Hilda, at fourteen, was the youngest of the family. She bid me farewell with such little emotion, I thought she was secretly pleased to have my parents all to herself. I felt a twinge of jealousy.

Heber, my brother, came all the way from the "States" to accompany me on this journey. He's a jolly looking round-faced man and I watched him hold his tears back and hug everyone. Heber has one leg shorter than the other, and it gave him a bit of a swagger as he walked. He wore a thick elevated shoe on one foot as a result of childhood polio. The shoe was custom made of dark brown leather and had been expensive. We made our hurried good-byes and Heber directed me to a small shelter and the awaiting dog sled.

A team of large black Newfoundland crossbred dogs stood hitched to the sled. They yipped and snapped at each other playfully. When the driver walked over they settled down eager for work. They had a long icy pull ahead. As we waited to load our luggage, I took one last look at my dear hometown of Twillingate. The few shops we had were still closed at this early hour. I moved about trying to stay warm, the snow underfoot had a crisp, crunchy feel.

The driver was a local villager by the name of Graham. I watched closely as he stacked and strapped our baggage to the toe of the sled. Two young ladies from "Round the Bay" were already settled in at the back of the sled.

Heber and I climbed in and snuggled under two thick woolen blankets. We gave a brief hello to the two young ladies. It was too cold to dilly-dally today. A crisp, cold breeze made the temperature dip, the sun was bright as it broke through a bank of morning cloud cover. The offshore wind was chilly for this time of year.

The dogs were eager to get running. It would be a long journey across the frozen snow and ice before we reached the mainland of Newfoundland.

Timid by nature, I normally would have been terrified by such a journey, but I felt safe with Heber. I prayed and made my peace with God. I was determined to replace fear with thoughts of adventure. There was no turning back.

The eight burly dogs dug into the snow and pulled the sled away from the shelter. I waved farewell to my family until they were no longer visible. The town of Twillingate began to move away, smaller and smaller until it too disappeared. We were enveloped in silence, except for the crunch of the frozen snow and ice beneath the sled's runners.

The biting cold whipped at my face. I pulled my cap over my ears, and tugged the woolen blanket tighter, up over my nose. I wore my seal skin cap and boots, a present from Father. He made them from the thick hide of the seals he hunted on the ice floes last winter.

Fishing and hunting were the livelihood of the village men. My father was one of the best. Always a hard worker and smart, he provided well for us. He sold his daily catch of fish, mostly haddock and cod, seal meat, and skins to passing freighters and passenger ships. They landed in Twillingate to stock up on provisions and goods, and my father provided them.

"Mush, mush on there," the driver called to the team. The sled glided bumpily across the ice towards the mainland, and my thoughts drifted to island life in Twillingate, and the earlier days of my upbringing.

Photo on page 4
James and Elizabeth Primmer in Twillingate

CHAPTER 2

ISLAND LIFE

1900 - 1927
GLADYS

Life on the island of Twillingate was simple but good. Both my parents were of British descent. I heard rumor that my mother Elizabeth carried a trace of the Beothuk Indian in her bloodline. The Beothuks were indigenous to the island of Newfoundland. Twillingate was discovered first by the Vikings, then the French, followed by the English, Spanish, and Italians, as well as pirates of days gone by.

The island's original name Toulinguet is French; it later became anglicized to Twillingate. With its good harbor and proximity to rich fishing grounds it was one of Newfoundland's greatest fishing ports.

The native Beothuk managed to survive in small numbers until the early 19th century around Twillingate and the Exploits River. My mother bore a distant resemblance to the tribe, with her flat round face and sallow complexion. I was secretly pleased to think that we might be related to Shawnadithit, the last surviving female member of the Beothuk nation.

Shanawdithit was known for her native drawings. Sadly, she died in her twenties of tuberculosis in St. John's, Newfoundland. As the population grew, Twillingate became a prominent fishing community known as the *Capital of the North.*

I was the fourth of five children, four girls and a boy. Heber was usually pardoned from the heavy work because he had polio. Having extra time on his hands, he used to entertain himself with pranks and jokes, mostly besought upon his sisters. He once hid under our featherbed mattress and as we slept peacefully, he poked a long hatpin into the mattress until it hit its mark. The girls' screams only made the game more fun. Of course he was punished for his devilish tricks, but it didn't stop him from an occasional raid upon us.

"Are you okay there, Gladys?" Heber knocked me out of my daydreaming.

"Yes, thank you, Heber. Just a bit cold." He wrapped the woolen blanket around me tighter.

Our family home was sturdy, a typical outport saltbox. It backed up to a rocky cliff and faced the beach. It was our grandparent's home before it became ours. The kitchen was the center of activity, and the large wood-burning stove that kept us warm dominated it.

In my mind's eye I can visualize my mother in our kitchen. I watch her as she moves about the kitchen cooking, baking, and boiling water for tea. Cups of strong hot tea were always offered to our constant drop-in guests. Nestled on a bright sunflower platter there were a variety of biscuits, slices of fresh baked bread, and a jar of mother's homemade partridgeberry jam.

Constantly working, my mother Elizabeth was always there to oblige in her kind and quiet way. Sometimes my mother would be called in to midwife during a difficult birthing, and sometimes the babies died. In those days it was not uncommon for newborns to die during the hard times. Doctors were few and far between, and medical conditions were poor to none. Sometimes a doctor could do nothing to save a newborn with obvious birth defects.

My mother once described how the doctor set a malformed baby on an open windowsill, knowing it would not live. Death was considered a kindness in those harsh times.

The bitter cold from riding in the sled across the ice soon brought me back to the present.

CHAPTER 3

DAILY CHORES

1900 - 1926
GLADYS

I returned to my pangs of homesickness, but they soon drifted on to my parents and our family life. As long as I could remember there was work to do. Our chores included cleaning, caring for livestock, tending our gardens, or drying fish on the flakes. We walked out on the flakes, which were roughly built docks stretching into the ocean. My sisters and I gathered our father's catch and placed it on the flakes to dry in the sun.

Our mornings were filled with the smells of porridge and salt fish. We were allowed to have tea with three teaspoons of sugar. There were only a few cows on the island and we were blessed to own one of them. Her name was "Bessie." While most of the other villagers drank "tin" milk, we were lucky to have Bessie's fresh milk every day.

Morning started before sunrise and there were chores for everyone. We had chickens to feed and Bessie to milk. We also had "Paddy" our wonderful old dog; he looked like a Newfoundland that married a St. Bernard. We secretly fed Paddy scraps under the table. An old cat named "Puss" ran about the barn, and usually a litter of kittens darted under my mother's feet, begging for a bit of fish or a saucer of cream.

We had sheep too. Father usually walked up to the high pasture with Paddy to tend them. In early spring the sheep were sheared, and the wool carded to make into sweaters and blankets, socks and mittens. We washed the wool in Ivory flakes, and dried it by laying it out flat in a sunny spot in the garden. We all learned to knit early on and we passed away the freezing winter nights next to the fire and candlelight creating warm homemade garments.

We had a root cellar like most of the villagers; it was an essential part of island life on Twillingate. Vegetables, meat, and cheese were stored in our root cellar under the house. It kept our food from spoiling in the warmer months, and freezing in the colder months.

When our chores were done, we left straight for school. I always finished up my chores quickly, for I loved school dearly and never wanted to miss a day. There was only a one-room schoolhouse for the entire village of children. I was generally a shy child, but not at school.

"She's some smart," the villagers commented, meaning very smart. I memorized and recited poems and plays, and put on skits for the class. I could read with ease, and do figures faster than anyone in the class.

My sister Susannah and I were best friends. Chubby, Sue had a flat round face and a mane of deep carrot-colored hair with freckles as big as peas. We were opposites. I was skinny as a pole bean, with a nose too big for my long face. Sue had brilliant ginger hair where mine was just plain brown.

God lingered in Twillingate when we were growing up. We were raised in His shadow. Sundays were devoted to Him. We attended church in the morning, after lunch, and again in the late afternoon. We belonged to the Methodist Church, and my father read the bible on Sunday evenings. We said grace at every meal. Usually grace was short and to the point, "God bless this food, which now we take, to do us good for Jesus sake. Amen." Another custom during the winter months was Mummering. Neighbors would dress in disguise and visit the homes of their friends and neighbors. It was the custom to have a guessing game to determine the identity of the visitors. What fun when a lady turned out to be a man!

CHAPTER 4

ISLAND LIFE CONTINUED

1927
GLADYS

"Whoa!" the driver shouted to the team.

The sound of the sleddriver's voice jolted me back to reality. As we stopped for a few minutes break from the sled, I looked out onto the distant frozen sea. Our youth was made up of running along the beach on warm days, climbing pilings to watch the boats pass by, and sometimes jigging for cod or squid off the flakes. We also threw nets for smelts. In the summer the beach stank of "blubber barrels." These wooden barrels were filled with cod liver oil and strung alongside the cod shacks. I was leaving that way of life behind forever.

The sled pushed onward through the open, barren land-scape. Lost in thought again, I bundled the blankets around me. Heber's eyes were shut, and as I closed mine again, I could see our huge garden near the house. I saw Mother bent over her vegetable patch, her round cheeks glistening and her nose red with the cold. She would be planting soon, or digging up last year's potatoes. Mother did whatever it took to produce enough to can or store for the hard winters that loomed so quickly after harvest. There would be cabbages, potatoes, carrots, turnips, and onions. We were lucky to have such a fine garden.

Father had a barrel of apples and half a tub of molasses. In the spring when all the molasses was gone, the sediment on the bottom of the barrel was sweet like molasses candy. When summer arrived we would go picking for partridgeberries and blueberries, and have a picnic. The berries were my favorite.

"Eh there, Gladys, okay there? We're about halfway now." I

nodded and put a brave face on it. The ladies in the back were quiet, one had her eyes closed while the other fiddled with her gloves. I fell to reminiscing again.

I remembered the stories of our Grandfather Primmer. Descended from good English stock, he had a decidedly Irish cast. His red hair and grand stature enhanced his strong face and stocky, muscular build. Many years before I was born, Grandfather Primmer had created the finest potato garden on the island. When the ships came in from Europe, he would walk his wheelbarrow down to the beach to where the ships had dumped mounds of rich soil.

The soil was originally used as ballast to weight the empty vessels - empty because the ships came to fill their hulls with goods from the island. Twillingate soil consisted mostly of rocks, with the thinnest and poorest layer of earth stretched over the outcroppings. After years of pushing his wheelbarrow from the beach, our garden lay deep in the rich European soil Grandpa had so laboriously carted. Those who were too shortsighted to do the same envied my grandfather's foresight.

As we plowed ever onwards to our destination, I looked forward to the milder climate of the states. Summer in Twillingate meant haying season. As Father hayed the fields he raked it into large mounds. Mother and all us children piled it up on bed quilts, rolled them up, and carried them back to the barn. Sometimes we used a small cart, pulling it, pretending we were goats or ponies. There were very few horses on the island back then, just a few Welsh ponies that were brought over on barges.

The ocean was such an essential part of our lives, but oddly enough most of the locals didn't know how to swim. Casualties by drowning were immense. Imagine spending your life in a dory, fishing out your livelihood, bobbing about in a vast sea like a cork, with a storm brewing on every white cap, helpless to save yourself if cast overboard. Many a fisherman had been swallowed up needlessly in the vast depths of the ocean. It may be that the frigid waters were just not inviting enough to learn to tread water.

CHAPTER 5

STORYTELLING

1926
GLADYS

This was a trip of a lifetime for me really, and already I felt homesick. How was I ever going to survive the change? We had been up at the crack of dawn, and I soon found myself lulled back into a relaxing slumber-like daydream about one of my favorite subjects - Storytelling!

There was always storytelling in my family. One of my favorites was the one Mother would tell about Puss. My mother had never been one to tell a lie. Once we had a calico cat named Puss and she had a penchant for getting her nose into things she had no business in.

Mother would milk Bessie and let the milk stand to allow the cream to come to the top. The milking buckets would be covered with linen towels, and my mother was never very far from the milk, but Puss was not far from it either.

"Go away with you, Puss!" Mother would shout.

The cat was forever being caught, trying to lick the rich cream off the top of the milk buckets, until one day Mother, dear and kind as she was, had enough. She grabbed Puss by the scruff, put her in an old burlap sack, and rowed out into the harbor a fair piece, and with all her might she flung the burlap bag with the cat in it overboard.

She rowed back to shore, worrying the whole way that it was a most terrible sin to have drowned the cat. By the time Mother got back to shore, that cat was sitting there waiting to greet her!

Mother said, "That's as true as I was born to die." So it must have been true. Puss lived to a ripe old age and licked the cream whenever she thought no one was looking.

Although I was really too young to remember the great maritime disaster, Titanic, I did remember the stories. It happened in April 1912, and I was about four at the time. Every spring, icebergs travelled the waters off Twillingate before melting into the warmer waters south of Newfoundland. Only four hundred nautical miles east of Cape Race, the great ship Titanic hit one of these huge floating icebergs, and sank to the bottom of the sea. Despite multiple attempts from the village of Heart's Content to cable the Titanic of the danger, sadly, it was all to no avail.

The Trans-Atlantic Cable they used was built in 1866, and ran under the ocean from Heart's Content to England. It was quite the pride and joy of Newfoundland.

I also remember hearing stories about the SS Florizel maritime disaster of 1918. The Florizel was a flagship for Bowring Brothers Red Cross line. The steamship was specifically built and designed to navigate the icy waters off Newfoundland and considered a luxury liner. The Florizel headed out of St. John's harbor on a voyage to New York, and crashed full speed onto a reef head at Horn Head Point. Only forty-four of the 138 passengers survived.

Perhaps the saddest tale was the loss of Betty Munn, only three years old. Her family erected a statue of her favorite character Peter Pan at Bowring Park, St. John's, in her memory.

Still vivid in my mind is another story my family spoke of, a local shipwreck. Some of the survivors drifted to the shores near Twillingate. The villagers along the coast took the passengers in. They were near frozen, some in shock, and others barely alive.

To the children remembering the scene, the survivors appeared as frozen as the sea they came from. One of my dear friends who was twelve at the time described three of the survivors, all women, sitting at her kitchen table staring at the steaming cups of tea set before them, silent, and lost in their grief. News of the survivors was telegraphed to New York and three days later a freighter arrived to gather the living and bury the dead.

My sister Susannah and I waded into the icy waters of the bay to pluck floating oranges and small wooden crates filled with the fanciest tins of food, wreckage from ships that shared the same fate as Titanic. To us, the bay was filled with floating treasures. We were far too young to understand the tragedy attached to our bounty. It was well worth a dip in the cold water, my sister said.

CHAPTER 6

ENTER GORDON

1927
GLADYS

As a teenager growing up in Twillingate, I was hired on to work as a salesclerk at Clark's store. As I sat in the sled, I considered that I probably would have stayed in Twillingate doing book-keeping and sales if not for Heber's generosity so I could go with him on this great adventure to St. John's and the United States.

"Whoa now! Whoa," shouted Graham to the dogs. Finally, after what seemed like an eternity, the dog sled had reached land. We were directed to a small private home, and had a short rest and a light lunch, before boarding the train to St. John's. Mother had wrapped a parcel in string. Inside it was her homemade cherry cake, heavy enough to sink the Titanic, and rich with home churned butter, candied cherries, and of course baked with love.

Heber and I carved off small slices and ate it with our tea.

"Some good cake," said Heber, wiping crumbs from his chin.

Yep, and better because Mother made it, I thought.

We heard the train whistle blow and hurried with our bags to board the train to St. John's.

What a wonderful sight the train was. Inside there were comfortable bench seats covered in dark leather, and wide windows to look out on the scenery as it raced by us. Our train clattered along the tracks, steaming through small fishing villages, the barrens, rocky landscapes, and along the shoreline until the city of St. John's appeared.

St. John's was not much of a city back then, but as it loomed out of the rocks and cliffs, the hills and steep streets made it appear much larger than it really was. It was the greatest city I had ever seen. We gathered up our baggage and dragged it up the hill of Bowery Street.

"I wish I could help you, Heber, but I'm having a hard time myself with this load," I said out of breath.

Finally we reached the doctor's office. I had to be inoculated before I could enter the United States. It was here, as we sat waiting our turn, that we met Gordon Harnum. Gordon sat on the edge of his chair, chatting animatedly to Heber about Boston and the possibilities there for work. Gordon had a shock of blond waves and eyes the color of the sky. I just couldn't help but stare at those blue eyes. Too shy to enter into the conversation, I just sat there with a pleasant smile, nodding when it seemed appropriate, and smiling more when Gordon glanced my way.

He was handsome, in a rugged way. He and Heber were getting along great. Their conversation switched back and forth between whispered secrets to abrupt bursts of laughter. Private jokes, I thought. I sat there lost deep in my own thoughts, but with one ear still listening to the conversation of the two men.

"Gladys Primmer!" I jumped up when my name was called.

My exam complete, I received my certificate to travel and I was pleased when Gordon decided to continue our visit on the ship to Boston.

We boarded the ship S.S. Rosalind, part of the Furness Red Cross Line fleet, not a particularly grand ship, functional at best. But to me it was the means to the "Promised Land," and as grand as any ship I'd ever traveled on. I had never been far from the shoreline in Twillingate, and then only in a dory. I couldn't swim, and the fear of falling over into the sea kept me close to shore.

The ship was large enough to carry hundreds of passengers, and looked quite capable of withstanding any storm. We went below and I surveyed our cabin, all 8 x 6 feet of it. I tried not to think of it as the claustrophobic tomb that it felt.

The journey would take a part of the day and the seas looked quiet. But soon after the ship embarked, the seas began to swell and toss, rolling and pitching the ship. I clutched the handrail as if my life depended on it and made my way back to our cabin. Heber stayed with me through the worst of the storm. Holed up in that tiny cramped cabin with our lifebelts on, I silently prayed we would live to tell the story.

"Lord Jesus, save us," I heard Heber pray out loud. We both lay on the bottom bunk, but sleep eluded us.

After a stormy start, the day brought bright sunshine and calm seas. A walk on the deck to breathe some fresh air connected us again with our new friend.

"Hey, boy, I see you lived through the storm!" said Gordon, smiling.

"Thought we were goners," remarked Heber light-heartedly. He looked at me and I cringed a little, because at least I really thought I was a goner.

"Yes, rough enough to last me a good long time," Gordon nodded. "We'll soon be in Halifax, get our sea legs, and then on the train to Boston for me. Will you be travelin' to Boston yourself, Heber?"

"Yes, my sister is anxious to get settled. She's staying with Fannie and me for a few days, and then she'll be at our sister Sue's for a bit. This is Gladys's first time in the States. We have another sister, Lucy . . . Luce, in New York, and she may stay there too."

"Gladys wants to look for a job in New York City and she's looking forward to visiting with her. Luce has been gone from home the longest. She works like a dog at a hospital, and her husband can't find work, but I think it's because of the drink. He's a hard man, poor Luce."

I had listened quietly to the conversation. I had nothing to add, so I said nothing.

Gordon turned directly to me and caught my eye and winked. As cold as it was on deck, I felt a flush rise from my face and warm my insides.

"Maybe I could take you out to a picture show in Boston? Have you ever been?"

"No, never," I was too embarrassed to say it, so I looked to Heber for support. He gave me a grin and said, "Sure, Glad would enjoy it. Thanks, that would be great, I'll give you our address and you come on over sometime after Glad has settled in." Gordon agreed to that enthusiastically and he winked at me again. A chill went up my spine and I shivered.

Excited, I excused myself to the cabin to gather our belongings, we would soon be there. A faint outline of the coastline of Halifax appeared before us and shortly we arrived. Once we reached port Heber hastily moved me off the ship to the dock.

"Get a move on, Gladys, or we will be here for days." We shifted our heavy baggage from our hands to the ground, and pushed them forward with our feet, as the line moved ever so slowly through Customs.

We were soon out of Customs and on the streets of Halifax.

Shops lined both sides of the street, and I could only wonder what lovely things were in them. I paused to look at some chocolates in a shop window. They looked delicious.

"No time to dilly-dally, Gladys. We have to catch the Boston bound train."

"Okay, Hebe."

Catching my reflection in a shop window, I couldn't believe how disheveled I looked. I pressed my hands down over my skirt to flatten the wrinkles.

"Taxi!" Heber hailed a cab.

The excitement had worn a bit thin after hours of traveling. A hot cup of strong tea and a cooked meal was the only day-dream wandering in my thoughts.

We climbed onto the train with considerably less excitement than the first train ride. But the rocking and the clickety-clack soon lulled us into slumber. Exhausted, we slept through the speeding darkness pressed into the corners of the leather seats, our coats balled up for pillows. I sat dreaming of my new life in America.

Photo on page 16
Gordon Hedley Harnum 1920s

CHAPTER 7

HEART'S DELIGHT

June 1911
Trinity Bay, Newfoundland

Two young boys stood on the tall rocky cliffs overlooking
Trinity Bay. They watched the village fishermen in their dories
hauling in their nets. It was the end of the day, and the nets
were full of cod. There was a silence. No gulls flew over the
water. Normally the boys climbed over the rocky cliffs to the
tidal pools. In the smooth rocks below they would search for
small fish and sea urchins that got trapped till the tides returned.
Not today. They watched the dories heading back to the distant
shore and their homes. The fog had rolled in early. One dory
remained rocking in the waves. It was too far out to see anyone
and the fog moved in quickly. The sun would soon be setting
and the air was getting colder so they turned around and headed
for home.

CHAPTER 8

NORTH STATION, BOSTON

1927
GLADYS

"North Station, North Station!" shouted the conductor in a nasally Boston accent.

"We're here, Glad," my brother sang out. We disembarked in a tumble of energy and expectation. The station was fascinating, filled with lights, noise, and shouting. I loved the hustle and bustle. I watched eagerly as passengers ran to catch last minute connections, while others waved fond farewells to loved ones. The tall clock tower struck noon as I stepped out of North Station and into the sunshine of Boston.

"There's Sue and Frank up ahead," my brother waved frantically. My sister Sue and her husband Frank Jenkins were there to meet us. Sue's husband worked as a carpenter. They lived in Somerville. Heber's wife Fannie was there to meet us and help with the bags. They had a car too, what a surprise!

As we walked out of the train station I heard shouting from the men selling goods. "Newcomers, newcomers!" they shouted.

I blushed, "Oh, Sue, how do they know I'm a newcomer?"

Sue gave a hearty laugh. "Glad, they're selling cucumbers!"

Embarrassed because I didn't understand their thick Boston accents, I laughed with her. We all squeezed into an old Dodge touring car that had seen better days. I jumped back into the rumble seat with Fannie. Always the life of the party, she gave a loud whoop, and we were off! Fannie was wonderful, always full of laughter and fun to be around.

She's a good match for him, I thought, and a great cook too, lucky Heber.

CHAPTER 9

A VISIT FROM GORDON HARNUM

1927
GLADYS

I had been at Fannie and Heber's about a week when Fannie called me one evening from my room.

"GLADYS! There's a phone call for you," she hollered, a big grin on her face. "It's Gordon Harnum."

She had heard the story about Gordon from Heber. I was too shy to bring it up myself, but I couldn't hide my smile as Fannie handed me the phone.

"Hello, Gordon, what a surprise!" I exclaimed.

"Did you think I'd break my promise to take you to the picture show?" I could tell he was teasing me, but I'd never had a date in my life. I felt flattered, nervous, and pleased all at the same time.

"Oh yes, please, that would be wonderful! How kind of you." I must have sounded about eight years old.

"I'll take the trolley to your brother's, if they don't mind me taking you out. How's Saturday night at six? The movie starts at eight but we can visit awhile so your family feels comfortable with me."

I handed the phone over to Heber, they chatted awhile, and he gave Gordon the address and directions. Saturday took forever to arrive.

"Hurry up now, he'll be here soon," Fannie chided me.

"Really, you should get yourself a Marseille wave. It's all the rage. I just love mine."

Blushing, I looked into the mirror.

"Oh, I don't know if it's really me."

"Of course it is. You're in America now, Glad!" She gave me a supportive hug.

I stared at my reflection in the mirror and thought, What on earth can he see in me? I am not just thin but ninety pounds of thin. He knows I'm well educated, and I think he enjoys that. I'm Godly and being a Newfie, he was probably raised the same way.

In fact, all the Newfoundlanders I knew went to church. Really, it was our only social event, with the exception of an occasional birth, death or marriage.

I continued my self-scrutiny and smiled into the mirror. My teeth were white and straight. My deep blue eyes and sweet smile seemed my strong points. My reflection impudently stuck her tongue back at me. "Yes, that too, I have a tongue that can carry on a decent conversation, if it's something I know about. I'm not very worldly though," I sighed.

As I continued to study the mirror, my reflection pulled a haughty face at me. As I was inspecting this new result, Fannie came by and looked me over.

"You look a proper lady. You'll be fine. If you're tongue-tied, let him do the talking." Which later on I found to be great advice.

Gordon arrived at six o'clock sharp. He looked handsome in a brown herringbone jacket; the scent of tobacco and the city entered the room with him. We all gathered in the small sitting room. They wanted us to get to know each other better.

I felt embarrassed, it was difficult for me to even look at Gordon, never mind carry on a conversation. He looked so handsome, with that shock of blond waves. His piercing blue eyes made me want to look away. Fannie kept winking at me and I'm sure I blushed ten to the dozen.

"So Gordon, tell us a bit about yourself," said Heber. "We're all from different parts of Newfoundland. What part are you from?"

"Oh, I'm from Heart's Delight in Trinity Bay. I can remember back vividly to when I was about six years old," Gordon said.

"Six? What happened back then?" We looked at him inquiringly. Being Newfoundlanders, we were naturally curious and we all loved a good story.

"Well, my father died see, and I was only six years old. He was a fisherman and I was in school at the time."

"You were in first grade?" asked Heber.

"No, not first grade," Gordon thought about it. "At least we didn't call it first grade. More like a kindergarten."

"So anyways, I was at school see, and my father, he was a fisherman, like most Newfoundlanders. But Pa was allergic. No, no, that's not the right word. He had epileptic fits. On that particular day, he went out in the dory alone. The fishermen had long come in. They saw him out there and he seemed to be okay. After being on shore for a while, the other fishermen began to wonder where he was and why he didn't show up. They climbed the hill overlooking the bay. His dory was anchored out in the same place. So a few men rowed back out in their boats to check up on him."

Gordon gave a slight choking sound and averted his eyes.

"When they got to him he was face down in his catch of cod. He smothered to death from an epileptic seizure. Later, they brought his body back in. A cousin of mine came to the school to get me and my brother Bill and take us home."

The room went quiet, and we all sat in suspense. I suddenly felt cold. A shiver ran down my spine as he continued his story.

"That was June of 1911, and my mother wasn't doing too well. She lasted a little over two years and passed away from pneumonia when I was eight. It was a hard time. When she passed, she left us more or less penniless and orphaned."

"My brother and I have one sister, Eva. So she promised she would do the best for us and she did. She was about nineteen at the time, and not long after my mother passed, she married a fellow named Ambrose Perry. Ambrose worked laying track down for the new railroad. He was kind and promised to support us, and we could stay in our family home," Gordon explained.

Speechless, I sputtered, "Oh, Gordon, how tragic, both your parents gone by the time you were eight?"

"Yes, but we were lucky we had our sister Eva. She gave up her life for us."

Quickly, he said. "We should get going or we'll miss the picture show."

"Oh yes, yes. I'll just get my coat."

I grabbed my serviceable navy wool, embarrassed because Gordon looked very dapper in his tweeds. We walked to the trolley stop at Inman Square. The movie house was near the Boston Common.

"Have you been to downtown Boston since you arrived?" he asked.

"No, we went to Heber and Fannie's place right off," I replied.

Gordon gently held my arm as we crossed the busy street. It was a thoughtful gesture. We watched *Charlie Chaplin vs. The Revolving Door,* a black and white silent movie. Charlie Chaplin, a popular comedian back then, played a chap that had too much to drink and got stuck in a revolving door. He kept going around and around in the hotel door. Each time the doorman tried to throw him out, Chaplin fell right back into the door and started going around in circles again. It was hilarious and the whole theater was laughing.

Gordon and I laughed till tears rolled down our cheeks.

Gordon bought us a sleeve of popcorn, another first for me. It was buttered and salty and very good, but I didn't eat much. I thought I'd choke on the kernels, we laughed so hard.

"So, did you enjoy your first picture show?" he asked as we walked side by side down the street.

"Yes, it was funny," I said still laughing. "I have so much to write and tell my family. I really miss everyone back home."

We walked through Boston Common talking about Newfoundland and laughing about the silly way we said things, and the names of things we were used to.

Gordon smiled and said, "Like the village I'm from is called Heart's Delight, and the next village is Heart's Desire, and the next village is Heart's Content." We both laughed at that.

"Yes," I said. "Life in Twillingate was good, so safe and simple. I miss my parents and Hilda, but I'm here now and what a great adventure it is."

On the trolley ride home, Gordon asked when I'd be going to New York.

"Next week, I think. I haven't seen my sister Lucy in a few years and I want to get a job there."

"Well, I hope you'll come back to visit. New York isn't for everyone," he said. "I'd really like to see you again."

I know I blushed, but I spoke right out, "Yes, I'd like that too."

Gordon said he would write, and I said I would do the same.

Two weeks with my family flew by and all of a sudden it was time to leave. My next stop, New York! I planned to stay with my sister Lucy in Brooklyn and look for a job. That morning I boarded a train headed to New York City.

CHAPTER 10

NEW YORK

1927
GLADYS

Lucy stood on the platform waving as the train pulled in. It was so good to see her I couldn't hug her enough. She looked older and somehow quieter, almost somber.

She had married a fellow named Steve Sweetapple, a Newfoundlander. I had never met him and I hoped he wouldn't mind me staying with them, at least for a little while. We arrived at their apartment, a three-story walk-up in the Bronx in one of the many brown buildings. They had their own bathroom with a sink and toilet, but no bathtub. The tub sat down the hall and they shared it with the other tenants. The landlady, a Mrs. Malone, was a friendly old soul and said we could use her phone in an emergency. She was maybe forty, prematurely gray, with a young daughter. There was no mention of a husband and no one asked.

At the time I moved there, Lucy worked as a dietician at Mercy Hospital. She worked long hours and had to walk a good part of the way there and back. She was thin like me, and we favored each other in looks. Steve was a carpenter but he had little work. Most of the work going then was out on Long Island.

"The rich are building mansions there," he told me. "I don't have any way of getting there, no car and no way to carry my tools."

Steve looked discouraged and I noticed he drank some.

I slept on a cot in their hall. The building was noisy, tenants coming and going, doors slamming. The smell of boiling cabbage permeated the stairwell. The noise of the horns from the street below kept blaring, yet that first night I slept deeply.

After a good night's sleep, and a hot cup of tea with biscuits under my belt, I decided to apply at Macy's for a job. I had my recommendation from Clark's Store where I worked as a clerk in Twillingate. I walked right into Macy's department store in New York City and twirled around in awe. How I wished my mother could see me now!

I asked the uniformed doorman where I could apply for a job. He smiled and winked at me, but he pointed me in the right direction.

I was soon hired as a window dresser. I would dress the mannequins and the window with the latest fashions and matching props. I enjoyed it. People would stop and stare at me through the window as I dressed the naked mannequins. I soon got over being embarrassed.

One day Lucy handed me a letter and smiled. I could see it was from Gordon. I ripped it open hurriedly. He was happy about my job, but he wondered if New York was really for me.

Six months flew by. I climbed the two flights of stairs to my sister's apartment one evening, every step heavy from the long hours I put in as a window dresser. Lucy was home early and greeted me warmly at the door. She smiled and her face was aglow with excitement.

"Oh Gladys, I'm so happy, I have some good news. I'm expecting a baby!"

I hugged her tight and kissed her. "Oh! I'm so happy for you, Luce. Does Steve know?"

"Yes, yes he does," she grinned. "He's hoping for a son."

I had so much to think about. There would not be enough room in the already cramped apartment with a new baby, and of course they would need time together as a family. As much as I loved my job, my wages were not enough for me to get a place on my own.

I didn't know anyone to room with, and New York was expensive for even the most modest of rooms. Maybe New York is not where I should be, I thought. Lucy begged me to stay and help with the new baby, but I needed to listen to my heart.

I decided to go back to Boston and stay with my sister Sue until I could find work there. Sue was overjoyed at my return, and even better, I would have my own bedroom. Plus, I could visit Heber and Fannie; they were only a short distance from Sue. Laura, my childhood friend, lived in the same area with her husband. And then of course there was Gordon. It all seemed to make perfect sense to me.

I wrote to Gordon the next day. "I've decided to return to Boston."

I received a reply soon after by telegram. It said, "Will come to New York and ride the train back with you –STOP- Acknowledge if you are in agreement. Gordon."

And I was, of course, I was!

Photo on page 28
Lucy Primmer Sweetapple and her husband Steve

CHAPTER 11

RETURN TO BOSTON

1927
GLADYS

I met Gordon coming off his train at Grand Central Station. We had two second-class one-way tickets to Boston. We boarded and found a carriage all to ourselves. On the ride back, Gordon, who liked to reminisce about his past, settled back in his seat. The warm glow of the carriage lights set the scene as he continued to tell his tale about his parents' death and his struggle to survive in Newfoundland.

"At first Eva did the best she could for us and the local villagers came by and helped some. But also, they borrowed all my father's tools and equipment until there was nothing left, and nothing was ever returned. About six months after my mother passed away, Eva married Ambrose Perry. Poor Eva, it was not out of love she married, but necessity. She married Ambrose and kept her promise to us. She kept Bill and me out of the orphanage."

"At eight, I wanted to help out, so I went to work at the sawmill breathing sawdust all day. I worked one summer and went back to school in the fall. I went to school till I was ten. At fourteen I went away, not to say that I ran away, but I just went away to look for work."

I listened to Gordon. His blonde hair dipped over his forehead and shadowed the pain in his eyes as he talked about the past. I felt at ease with him even though I hardly knew him.

Gordon rambled on in a comfortable chatter.

"I went to my uncle first to borrow money, see? I needed a loan in the amount of twenty dollars. I came back discouraged and told my sister I couldn't get the money."

"Then what happened?" I encouraged him, although he hardly needed any encouragement.

"Well, I happened to tell my story to a fellow by the name of Harve Jacobs, whom I hardly knew. I told him that I had a mind to go look for work. I told him I had tried to borrow money from my uncle but he didn't want to loan it to me. Well, to my surprise Harve reached into his back pocket, pulled out an old worn wallet, and took out a crisp twenty-dollar bill."

"He said, 'You go ahead and take it. If you can pay me back, all right. If you can't, I'll never miss it anyways.'"

"So I got the money, and I went away to find work. I traveled over three hundred and fifty miles from home at the age of fourteen to pick and shovel. I dug trenches fourteen feet deep in Grand Falls, Newfoundland."

"That must have been horrible, Gordon."

Gordon paused and looked at me. "Sorry, I talk too much."

"Not at all," I smiled back at him. "Your childhood was so unlike mine but you certainly survived it well." I yearned to hold him in my arms and run my fingers through his forelock. Instead, I just sat there smiling at him.

Gordon looked down at my neatly folded hands. He placed his hands over mine. I froze, but I didn't say a word. My heart pounded as hard as the locomotive that carried us.

"Gladys, I came here to travel back with you in hopes that you would marry me."

He looked deeply into my eyes as the train gained speed and plunged us into the night.

His piercing blue eyes seemed to penetrate into my very soul. I jumped up out of the seat so quickly I nearly banged my head on the overhead.

"Yes, Gordon, yes I will. Yes!" He wrapped me in his arms and kissed me, and I responded with real passion.

CHAPTER 12

THE WEDDING

1927
GLADYS

I glanced up at Gordon as the train got closer to Boston. He looked quite pleased with himself. Maybe I had been too hasty.

"You should have asked Heber for my hand first," I smiled, trying to gain a little ground.

"Oh," he smiled right back at me, "but I did."

"Heber said we were well suited and gave me his blessing. He didn't tell you because he didn't want to influence your decision. He said you were wise enough to make your own choices."

Well, that's true enough, I thought.

Shortly after that, the train pulled into North Station, Boston. I was no longer so awed by the activity of the vendors peddling their wares. My time in New York City had cured me of that. I even chuckled when I thought about the cucumbers-newcomers mistake. Our eyes were assailed by the bright sunlight after the cool dimness of the station. Once they adjusted, we saw Heber waiting proudly by his touring car parked at the curb.

"Hey Boy, whadda y'at? How was the trip?"

"Well Heber, I asked your sister to marry me."

We were barely seated in the car when Heber asked, "Gladys, are you happy?"

"Yes," I grinned, "I am happy, very happy."

We got in the car and dropped Gordon off near his flat on Proctor Road. Gordon hugged me close.

"Goodnight, Heber, and thanks so much for the ride. I'll call you in the morning, Gladys." He nodded his head and touched my lips briefly. I watched him walk toward the darkness, his outline merging into the quickening dusk. Then he disappeared.

"Glad! Are you sure about this?" piped up Heber, snapping me out of my romantic musings and back to my senses.

"Yes, I am, but I'm also tired from the trip. I want to write to our parents as soon as we get to Sue's. I think I'll need a few days to let it all sink in. I know that you and Fannie are happy. I sure hope that Gordon and I will be happy too."

"Of course you will, Glad. Gordon is a good man."

It was at about the same time I wrote to my parents that I began to keep a journal. It was such a whirlwind romance I wanted to savor every moment of our time together. I stayed at Sue and Frank's house in Boston for the next few months. While I was there, I offered to help Gordon with bookkeeping for his various jobs. Time flew faster than a Newfoundland nor'easter.

Gordon and I were getting to know each other better. I enjoyed our small talk and banter. He had a good sense of humor, and could easily make me blush. We decided on a New Year's Eve wedding. Only a few months away, but I had plenty of time to invite everyone.

We agreed it would be a small affair, just family and a few friends.

December 24, 1927

My wedding is only a week away and I'm over-the-top with excitement. Soon I will be Mrs. Gordon Harnum! Fannie, bless her heart, has convinced me to have a Marseille wave for the wedding. So I did. Tight shiny waves fall in a crescendo over my left eye. I am still not convinced that it's any improvement. But she's so pleased and complimentary that I agreed just to be polite. Fannie and Sue helped me pick out a sensible outfit for the occasion. It's very practical in that Newfoundland way, but definitely not the most attractive dress. I tried it on today and took stock of my reflection in the mirror. Steady blue eyes peered back at me. The dress is a deep navy blue silk affair with a long jacket that falls to my hips. Only seven more days to go!

December 25, 1927

"Merry Christmas."

We clinked a toast with our glasses and chimed in. We had just finished a scrumptious Christmas dinner with Heber and Fannie, and we'd been discussing the church and my wedding service on New Year's Eve.

The service was scheduled at the historic St. James's Episcopal Church. Pastor Ernest Paddock would officiate. St. James's was located on Massachusetts Avenue in Porter Square, Cambridge. The church was on the National Register, a landmark structure with an arch of stained glass windows facing the avenue. Constructed in 1888, with generous contributions from Mary Longfellow, sister of the famous Henry Wadsworth Longfellow, St. James's was famous. It housed the historic bell re-cast by Paul Revere.

I was so pleased. My fondness for history made the church a perfect choice for our wedding!

A few weeks earlier, I had hand-printed simple invitations on card stock, cordially requesting the presence of our family and friends. The small guest list included Sue and Frank, Heber and Fannie, Gordon's brother Bill and his wife Violet. I also invited my best childhood friend Laura and her husband Lester. Luce and Steve recently had a baby, a boy named Donald. They sent their regrets to say they would not be able to attend. I was disappointed, but I understood the family burdens Luce faced.

December 28, 1927

Laura is coming! I am very fond of Laura, my childhood friend. She refuses to sound anything like a Newfoundlander and enunciates every word, never using any "Newfie" slang or the words "dis, dat, dem, or dose, my son, or yes maid." Lester works in maintenance at Harvard University, and they live in Harvard Square. They are in what is called a brownstone, just across Massachusetts Avenue from Harvard Yard.

Fannie plans to fire up a scoff, a real "down home dinner" of fish and brewis for after the ceremony. The fish will be salt cod and the brewis is hardtack soaked with turnips and potatoes. She promised to make a cherry cake with white icing. Knowing her, I'm sure there will be a plastic bride and groom on top. I should be nervous, but I'm just too happy. Only three more days to go!

NEW YEAR'S EVE

Finally the big day!

I sat in the bedroom humming to myself and looking through my meager trousseau when Sue entered. She looked serious and I wondered why. I thought she was going to say I was making a mistake.

"Gladys, there are things Mother never told us about marriage."

I smiled. "I think I know what you're going to say."

"No, you don't. I love Frank but sleeping with a man takes getting used to," Sue sighed and looked even more serious if that's possible.

"You might not like it but that's what comes with marriage. You will just have to make the best of it. Personally, I avoid it," Sue grimaced. Not a reassuring chat on my big day.

"Is it really so awful, Sue?

"It's a duty. Maybe you'll be all right with it." She dropped the subject because it was time to get ready. She helped me on with my dress and jacket.

"I think a bit of rouge on your cheeks, Glad." I had a hint of lipstick on, and I sat patiently while Sue dabbed gently with a puff of rouge on each check.

"Good enough, my girl. Heber will be here to pick us up soon. Let's get your trunk and cases ready to go." She smiled and her eyes lit up as she regained her excitement.

We arrived at St. James's right on time and I saw Gordon grin as I got out of the car. He stood waiting at the church steps. It was a cold day, but his jacket, unbuttoned, flapped in the wind along with the blue necktie I gave him as a wedding gift. Reverend Paddock went inside and instructed Gordon to wait at the altar.

The Reverend met me at the front door next and asked, "Miss Primmer, are you ready?"

"Yes. Yes, I am, Reverend Paddock."

"Then let's proceed," he said. Heber took my arm.

We followed Reverend Paddock as he walked down the long aisle with all due solemnity. Gordon's brother Bill, the best man, stood beside him. The ceremony was quick, and as we said our "I do's," Gordon gave me a polite kiss and took my hand. As we walked past our few family and friends, they turned and smiled upon us. We stepped out the door and a cascade of rice was thrown over us. Our new life as husband and wife had begun.

Fannie outdid herself with a fine down home dinner, and of course there stood the plastic bride and groom on top of the cherry cake. Heber had a bottle of our local Newfoundland Screech. I watched as he poured all the menfolk a small glass. He hesitated when he got to Lester and, instead of pouring, he looked to Laura.

I smiled as she pursed her lips and said, "Les, you better not.

We'd have to take the trolley home."

Heber raised his glass and proposed a toast to the new bride and groom. "Bless this marriage, may you both be happy and healthy and have many children." Les then played a jolly Newfoundland tune on his violin and we all clapped along.

Gordon sang,

"Oh, this is the place where the fishermen gather with fish lines and jiggers."

I was so pleased he knew the entire song. He could really sing quite well. We all laughed and cheered him on.

There were gifts from everyone. Fannie and Heber gave us money and a large cooking pot and four china plates with matching teacups. Sue and Frank made a present of towels and a blanket wrapped in blue ribbon. Laura and Les gave us a very generous amount of money, and Bill and Violet gave us six blue glasses with sailing ships etched in white. We needed everything, as we had almost nothing.

Finally, Heber drove us back to our new home, Gordon's rented two-bedroom apartment on Porter Road.

Now I was really nervous!

CHAPTER 13

HARD TIMES AHEAD

1928
GLADYS

I walked inside my new home. Gordon's apartment was laid with dark hardwood floors, dark stained woodwork, and white walls. The floors and walls were bare.

I must do something to brighten up this place, I thought.

The only furniture was a turned-up orange crate with two mismatched chairs. A large mahogany bed and an old scratched mahogany dresser that didn't match filled the bedroom. A small white table at the bedside held a wind-up alarm clock with two steel bells at the top. The bed had sheets, clean thank goodness, but no blankets or bedspread. The pillows looked flat.

"So Gladys, how does it feel to be Mrs. Harnum?" Gordon interrupted my thoughts on interior decorating.

"Oh, good I think, it's just that so much has happened in one day."

"Do you think you will grow to love me?" He grasped my hand.

"Yes, I can do that," I blushed.

"You must be tired and it's late. Long day. Thank goodness I won't have to look for work tomorrow. It's New Year's Day."

"I'll just get my nightgown and toothbrush and dress in the bathroom." I'm standing but my feet aren't moving. I heard sister Sue's warning in my head. Can it be as bad as she described? Might as well get it over with.

My sister never asked about that first night. I didn't tell her, partly because I thought it was romantic and not at all horrid.

JANUARY 1928

Monday came. It was only 4:30 a.m. I heard Gordon rummaging about in his sock drawer. I ran to the bathroom to brush my teeth and wash my face.

"I'll be right out to make tea," I shouted from behind the door.

"I'll only have tea and toast, no time for anything else," he shouted back.

I moved quickly to get the kettle filled. I had never used a gas stove before, and I watched with interest as Gordon pulled the wooden matches from a long box. He struck one match on the side of the box, and turned on the gas below the burner. I watched, fascinated as it burst into flames. I jumped back in surprise and Gordon grinned and caught me by the elbow.

I made him hot buttered toast, one slice of white bread on one side of the old fashioned toaster and another slice on the other side. Be careful not to burn it, I thought. Fannie had given us several jars of partridgeberry jam and I had a stick of butter, but only one stick. Food was becoming scarce and people talked of hard times ahead.

I heard Gordon as he busied himself in the bathroom. "Breakfast is ready," I shouted to the door.

"Be right out," he shouted back.

Being a wife can't be all that difficult, I think. He walked into the kitchen and ate his toast. He drank his tea quickly, scalding his mouth, and stifled an oath.

"I have a lot of walking to do today before I even get to the work line." He threw on his heavy navy pea coat, knitted cap, and wool gloves. I wanted to give him my scarf, but I thought he would refuse it. He wrapped his strong arms around me, and gave me a warm kiss, full of promise.

"I'll be gone all day. Pray that I find work."

"I will, I will," I said with enthusiasm and waved goodbye,

but I didn't see him look back.

I spent the day cleaning. I washed the wood floors and dusted the cupboards and windowsills. I placed our dishes, cups, and glasses in the cupboards. It barely filled two shelves. There were two pots - the large one Fannie gave us and the small one Gordon already had. There were tableware settings for four.

The most appreciated gift was the blanket. The apartment was poorly heated, and I was grateful for Gordon's strong warm body next to mine last night. Otherwise I think I would have frozen.

It was dark before I heard Gordon stomp up the steps. I was anxious to hear if he'd found work. The boom days of 1925 and 1926 were gone and I knew jobs were scarce. Thank goodness we didn't know about a fate worse to come, the Wall Street Crash of 1929.

I put a pot of hot soup on the stove and his favorite, homemade biscuits from scratch. Gordon put his coat on a hook at the entry and dropped his hat and gloves on the clanging radiator. It rattled and attempted to crank out some heat in greeting.

He looked very tired. He hugged me and sat down on one of our only two chairs.

"Tea? Would you like a cup of tea, Gordon?"

"Yes, that would be good, Glad, thanks," he said.

CHAPTER 14

AN UNEXPECTED SURPRISE

1928
GLADYS

I picked up my journal and studied it. It had been a while since I'd written. I sat next to the orange crate and went over past events in my mind since the wedding. Finally, I wrote.

February 15, 1928

Our first month has gone quite well considering all things. We are settling into the routine of married life. There's enough work for Gordon to pay the rent and keep food on our table, and I'm grateful for that. We're still quite frugal with our money and I pray that the unexpected news will be as welcome to Gordon as it is to me.

A few weeks ago I fell ill early one morning, the typical symptoms ensued, nausea and vomiting. I stuffed down a few saltine crackers and it went away. My mother was a midwife in Twillingate when I was growing up. I knew the first signs of pregnancy. I'm positive. I am pregnant! We've hardly been married. I think I must tell Gordon tonight, right away! He may not be happy about it, but I am definitely going to tell him tonight. Part of me is elated; the other part is scared. What will Gordon think? Oh, I hope he's pleased.

I closed my journal and prayed and then I crossed my fingers for luck.

Gordon tromped up the stairs to the apartment. He had a weary look on his face. I debated whether to tell him or not. After dinner I made some hot coffee with a few slices of lemon swirl. It was rich and sweet, I hoped to put him in a receptive mood.

Finally I got up the courage and told him the news. The look on his face worried me.

"Are you happy about a baby?" I asked.

"Oh, yes, it's just a grave responsibility and times are hard. We'll get by. Don't fret, Glad. I'm happy, I am," he said. He leaned across the orange crate to hug me.

Gordon didn't say it but I could see plainly what he was thinking, "How can we pay for a baby? We are barely scraping by now."

CHAPTER 15

GORDON SPEAKS

1928
GLADYS

We sat there by the orange crates and Gordon began to speak of his childhood. I knew some of his family history but I could see that he wanted to tell me some more, so I encouraged him.

"I was orphaned at eight. It was 1913 then, and my sister Eva raised my brother Bill and me. My childhood memories and recollections of our family all hang in this hallway." He brought in the family photograph off the wall. "That's a sepia photograph and it's still mounted in its original gilded frame."

I knew the photo he was talking about. I walked past it in

the hall a dozen times a day.

"That's my sister standing behind our parents." I looked at the photo; her hands were placed on her well-padded hips. Her hair was parted in the middle with plaits, curled back around into a small circle, and pinned at either side of her ears. Her face had a tight smile and her full figure was covered by a long sleeved dress with ruffles at the cuffs and neckline.

"That's my mother sitting in front with her hands in her lap. She had large hands and you can see the wear in them."

I see old hands on a woman with a young pretty face, hair pulled back into a neat brown bun, and a dress very similar to Eva's. In the photo his mother has a sweet smile, large kind eyes, and lovely high cheekbones.

"That's my father sitting beside her." He's a small wiry looking man with a mustache, and a nose far too big for his narrow face. He's wearing his wool cap and a wool waistcoat with a plain white collarless shirt beneath.

"My brother Bill was about eight in this photo." He looked the spitting image of his father without the mustache, and dressed in schoolboy short pants and long socks.

"I shared a likeness to my mother," he said.

I can see that, but Gordon had a rounder and more masculine face. He was quite fair back then with large eyes and a forelock of blond hair. He's wearing very short pants, unlike the long knee version that his older brother had on. Behind them in the photo is the front porch of the family home.

Gordon continued, "My father James Harnum was a fisherman, as were most men in the coastal village of Heart's Delight. My mother Sarah Wiseman was from a fishing family too, and their marriage was second for them both. My parents' marriage had been arranged. Seeing as both families were in the fishing business, it only made sense to join their son and daughter in matrimony."

"Both my parents had been widowed early, and it was a good business decision for both families. So James Harnum and Sarah Wiseman were wed. It was a twist of luck that they also loved each other."

Gordon continued, "My father suffered from epileptic seizures. Although he usually fished alone, the other fishermen were always nearby. You didn't need to trawl far from the shore to find fish in those days. His friends would give him a wave, and a shout, 'Are you all right, Jim boy?'"

"Father had a signal if he were in trouble. He would wave both hands back and forth if he was taken with a seizure, but on this particular day, the fog had rolled in early and his mates headed back to shore with their catch. They couldn't see my father waving both hands through the fog."

"When my father didn't return that day, it was a very bad sign. They found his boat in the mooring near the rocks, with his face down in his catch, suffocated in a pile of fish. Mother died two years later. Everyone said she died from a broken heart."

I had heard this story before and knew how painful it was for him. I held Gordon close in my arms. He had shared an important part of his past with me.

CHAPTER 16

FAMILY MATTERS

1928
GLADYS

Fannie loved to entertain, and she and Heber could afford to share their good fortune. Heber bought a six-family, three over three, house for three thousand dollars. It was a great place for the family to gather on the weekends. We would sit and chat about old friends from back home and about our parents. The men loved to keep some of the old Newfoundland stories alive. They were born storytellers and there was nothing they liked better than to tell the family tales, sometimes each one more outrageous than the next.

It was a short walk from my brother's house to Inman Square. Although it was an unattractive building, it always stayed rented and provided them a steady income. Heber, a talented carpenter despite his handicap, was successful and could usually outwork most of his fellow workers.

"Are you ready, Glad? We'll be late!"

"Yes, the blueberry pie is done. I'll just pack it up." We were headed to Heber's for dinner.

Gordon and I usually walked over to Heber and Fannie's for dinner on Sunday afternoons after church. Sue and Frank came over, and sometimes, Laura and Les came for Sunday dinner too. Gordon's brother Bill and his wife Violet went to St. James's Church and we often walked over together to Heber's.

We each brought a favorite dish and Fannie handled the main fare. After dinner, tea and dessert were handed around. Then the fun began. Story Time!

Childhood memories rushed out, tales true and not so true

came tumbling out as we passed the desserts around the table. Gordon especially loved to tell stories. He had so many interesting jobs since he was a young'un, and enjoyed recounting them in great detail. Heber and Bill occasionally interrupted him to make fun of something he'd said. We all laughed till we cried.

Tonight it was my turn to tell a story and I was just brimming with excitement fit to burst.

I blurted it out. "Great news! We're expecting a baby!"

"Well, well," piped up Fannie, overjoyed for us. "That was fast!"

Congratulations went all around the table, and I sat there grinning from ear to ear. My sister Lucy already had two children, Don and June. Sue has been hoping for children, but no sign yet.

As for Laura and Les? Not likely. Laura came from a family of thirteen and said she never wanted any children, not even a dog. I always felt bad for Lester because he loved both children and dogs. Bill and Violet were also expecting a baby soon, and although my pregnancy was unexpected I felt like the timing was good.

I was near my due date and our St. James's "church family" had been very generous. One of the parishioners gave us an almost new crib. The parish hall gave us a table they did not need, and a sofa they were replacing. We received a bounty of generosity from the group. We were so lucky we lived just across Massachusetts Avenue.

Kind churchgoers helped us carry everything across the avenue to our Porter Road home. I kept the house clean as a pin and rearranged the new furniture. Our first year was a challenge, but life was looking up and I felt happier than ever.

CHAPTER 17

THE GREAT DEPRESSION

On October 29, 1929 the Wall Street stock market crashed. Work and food were limited. There were breadlines and soup kitchens. People were hungry for food and work. Men stood waiting in lines, hoping for any kind of job.

October 1929
GLADYS

With the volume turned up loud on our radio, we heard the shocking news of the stock market crash. We heard the announcer say that people were jumping off ten-story buildings. It was like a nightmare and unimaginable to me.

There were stories of the very rich that had lost everything to the stock market who were now penniless, no better off than a beggar in the street. Thank goodness Gordon and I had no extra money to buy stocks. We knew that hard times lay ahead, the bread lines would be long, and the few scarce jobs would become even scarcer.

CHAPTER 18

THERE IS ALWAYS HOPE

1929
GLADYS

Gordon was ambitious and we were lucky he always found work. He was smiling when he came home from work one day.

"Glad, I stopped at that white church just the other side of Porter Square. Their steeple is in sorry need of paint. I gave the pastor a good price and he gave me the job."

"That's great news, but how will you do it? How will you paint a steeple?"

"I know just how. I can borrow a bosun chair from a man I know. I learned to tie knots from my mother while she was at the spinning wheel, and my father taught me to repair the fishnets. I'll do it when no one is looking. Otherwise the men on the street will watch me and take my job away. That is, if they are brave enough to hang off a steeple, ha-ha."

Even with the news of the crash and the Depression, my husband remained optimistic, especially since we had so little. In the days that followed food was in short supply. Churches handed out corn meal, margarine, powdered milk and sometimes flour, coffee and sugar. But amidst all that poverty somehow we flourished, and so did our first child.

CHAPTER 19

NEIL JAMES HARNUM

1928-29
GLADYS

Our first child Neil, called Jim, was indeed a handful. He had so much energy, and a temper to match that scared me. Gordon had little patience with him and I regretted that. One day he bit me while I was threading clothes through the wringer washer. It drew blood. Jim craved constant attention or he behaved badly.

"Don't worry, he'll outgrow it," everyone had told me. I couldn't wait.

I hadn't told Gordon yet, but I was with child again. I knew that this new development would add pressure to the current times. Plus now we had the worry of another mouth to feed and provide for. I worried that Gordon would be upset with me, and then just when I thought I could handle everything that was coming our way, I heard an unexpected bit of gossip from Violet.

Sister-in-Law Violet

At church one Sunday my sister-in-law Violet took me aside after the service.

"Gladys," she whispered in her tiny voice, "Bill told me that there were women hanging all over Gordon at the Green Parrot Pub. He's a looker and those women are not ladies."

It was true, my husband was extremely handsome, with ice blue eyes and a shock of blonde hair. I just couldn't believe he might be interested in other women.

I knew in my heart Violet was telling the truth, but her husband Bill was always a bit jealous of his brother Gordon.

Bill was a few years older, scrawny, and looked more like his father than his beautiful mother. He also had one skewed eye that would not look right at you, but went slightly off to the side.

I took this information from Violet with a grain of salt. I knew it was true but probably exaggerated. That night I mentioned Violet's conversation to Gordon.

"Aw, Glad, that's just plain foolishness. Just a few of the girls from back home in Heart's Delight and Carbonear, that's all. They stopped in for a whiskey and a chat with the boys from down home. No harm in that."

Wasn't there? I wondered. A deep grey unease had settled over me.

CHAPTER 20

SUICIDE OFF THE
CHARLES RIVER BRIDGE

November 1929
GLADYS

Life went on as usual with never a dull moment. A few weeks after the incident about Gordon at the Green Parrot Pub, there was a bridge jumper suicide. Less than a week later the police knocked on our front door.

"Mr. Harnum, may we speak to you?"

We had just been about to sit down to dinner. I had the baby in his high chair and I was fastening his bib. Gordon invited them in. The officers had Gordon's name from the police report, and they wanted to know what Gordon had seen that night at the Charles River bridge just before a man jumped to his death. Gordon had been on the bridge when it happened, so we knew the story.

Gordon told the officer he had been walking over the bridge with a friend and saw a man climb up the wall. He looked scared, as if he might jump.

"I shouted, 'Don't jump,' and I ran towards him, but he jumped anyways. You know, I can't swim a stroke, but I looked down into the water for him. The water was dark and he disappeared quickly, before I could see him. Then I ran to the street and stopped a car and told them to fetch the police."

"Could you give me the name of the person you were with to corroborate your statements?"

Gordon hesitated, "Her name is Rita Reed. I'll get her address for you. I don't know it right off."

Rita Reed! She was one of the girls from the Green Parrot

that Violet had mentioned. I was fuming. After the officers left, I turned to Gordon for an explanation. "What were you doing walking out with that redhead Rita Reed?"

"I just took her over the bridge to Boston, so she could look for work."

"How long have you been helping her find work?" This is the second time I had heard about Rita Reed. "I'm no fool, Gordon, and I won't put up with this behavior." I lashed out, angry and hurt at the same time.

"Gladys, c'mon, you're making a mountain out of a molehill. It's not what you think."

I felt my temper rising out of control. I said, "It might just be a good time for me to go back to Twillingate to visit my mother and father."

"What are you saying, Gladys? You're my wife and that's my child you're carrying. You need to calm down, Glad. You're not going anywhere," his blue eyes got frosty.

I spat back, "My mother is a midwife and has delivered many a baby and she can deliver mine too. It's a good time as any for a visit."

I shocked even myself but once the words were out, the decision was made. I wouldn't back down. Gordon knew about my stubborn streak.

"How long will you be gone? There's a depression going on and I need you here."

"I'll go just till the baby is born. Little Jim can meet his grandparents and his aunt Hilda."

"But that's a couple of months away!" Gordon groaned.

"Yes, it is. I'll make arrangements for my passage. I still have a little money saved over from when I worked in New York."

I was steaming with fury and covered with self-righteousness as I tromped out of the dining room. I wanted to let some of that steam out so I took baby Jim in the stroller over to see

Heber and Fannie. I told them that I was going back to Twillingate to have the baby. I had doubts about Gordon's being honest and faithful. They couldn't believe it.

I told them what Violet had insinuated at church, and that Gordon had been spending too much time at the Green Parrot, leaving me alone with the baby till sometimes after supper. Heber stuck up for my husband.

"I think Gordon is a good man, maybe he got a little ahead of himself. Men are guilty of enjoying the attention, and some women like to flatter men. Men like the attention. He's still young, he hasn't figured out married life yet, but I know he loves you."

"If you want to visit Ma, I'm all for it. But come right back after the baby is born. You married for better or worse and this will mend itself if you don't let it fester." Heber's words rang true.

I didn't say anything just then, but I decided I would follow my brother's advice and come back with the new baby. Gordon needed us and Lord knows we needed him.

1930s

CHAPTER 21

HOMEWARD BOUND

1930
GLADYS

I packed up the few things I owned for the baby and myself. I still hurt from Gordon's deception. I had to carry little Jim and I was already heavy with child, so I only took the barest necessities. The trip would be long and Jim wasn't one to be still. I had a rope tied around his waist when I wasn't carrying him. He could walk now, and I'd just pull him back when he got too far out of my control. I wasn't the only mother with a rope around her youngster's waist. It was a common practice back then.

I didn't have much of a singing voice but did my best to entertain Jim. I sang an old song that Father sang to us as children. "I love my doggie, my doggie loves me, I found him under the old oak tree. My little doggie goes bow wow wow, wow wow wow, bow wow wow. I love my kitty, my kitty loves me, I found her under the old oak tree. My little kitty goes meow, meow, meow" and so forth - a silly song, but he clapped and laughed.

The rest of the voyage was uneventful. I didn't see anyone from back home. But soon we were on the ferry to Twillingate and my heart began to lighten.

My father and mother were at the dock waiting for us when the small ferry arrived on the shores of my Twillingate home. It was joyous and sad. I felt so happy to be home again but racked by the pain of leaving Gordon. I looked around the harbor, it was the end of March and the ice had left the cove on the outbound currents. A few large icebergs floated off in the distance, and there was a nip of frost in the air and snow still on the ground. I was home!

CHAPTER 22

RETURN TO TWILLINGATE

May 1930
GLADYS

I've enjoyed being with my mother these last few months. I sat and watched her as she baked an old fashioned cottage loaf of bread and brewed us tea on the woodstove. I felt safe and loved and she waited on me knowing my time was near.

"No heavy lifting. The boy can walk now. It's good that your father has taken a liking to him and keeps him busy," Mother winked at me.

Father walked down to the shore almost every day with Jim. Today he brought a heavy reed basket and I watched as he and Jim gathered the smooth stones used to divide the flowers and vegetables and keep the weeds out. The stones on the shore were black or grey, smooth, and cool to the touch. The black ovals were my favorite as a child. Memories come flooding back to me. The sea had been tossing these stones upon the shore for a lifetime. A millennium of tidal motion had smoothed and shaped them. They held the secrets of the sea, my secrets.

Hilda had grown up since I left Twillingate and was dating a seaman. I watched as she flitted in and out of the house, running off to meet Peter. He's only a seaman, but has ambitions to be a captain one day.

"He loves me," Hilda sighed, "and I guess I love him too. You remember the Troake family. Mother and Father approve," Hilda boasted, pretending not to be in any hurry to marry.

"You'd be happy if he became a captain though. He'd be out to sea and you could still have some freedom."

"What do you mean?" she snipped at me.

"Just that a boring married life would not suit you," I smiled and hugged her. "Look at me having a second youngin' already."

"I wouldn't mind little ones," she said, "as long as they behave."

I knew she was referring to little Jim, and I couldn't blame her. He was a handful, but he was my handful. I looked to my mother, and she changed the subject.

I planned to name the baby Uldine Cavell Harnum if it's a girl, after the famous child evangelist. She will be quiet and patient and kind. If it's a boy, I've decided to name him Gordon. Jim was named after my father James. Gordon will be pleased that his son will be named after him. Gordon made me promise to call him as soon as I can, after the baby is born, but I wanted my parents to do that for me. I still felt hurt by Gordon's deception, but I felt embarrassed because I acted too hasty.

Gordon's called several times, wishing I were with him. It was easier to listen than talk.

"I have plans for a new business, as soon as I can get the money together I'm going to buy a truck."

"I'll tell you all about it when you get back with our new baby."

"Fannie's been over and set up a basinet stocked with lots of baby things."

"I shouldn't have told you. It was supposed to be a surprise. Act surprised!" Gordon sounded so happy, and I knew he was trying to make it up to me. I had a feeling that everything would work out just fine.

CHAPTER 23

A VISIT TO EVA

May 11, 1930
GLADYS

I went into labor today. Mother was calm and assuring. She did what she did best and I delivered a baby girl, Uldine Cavell. Gordon was anxious for my return and my father encouraged that.

"You've had a good visit. Your mother has delivered your little girl. You're welcome to stay but you belong back with your husband."

I had promised my husband before I left Twillingate that I would visit Heart's Delight to see his sister Eva and her husband Ambrose.

Gordon called me soon after, "As soon as you're ready Eva wants to see you and my little ones."

I packed my bag making sure I had plenty of nappies and a change of clothes for the three of us and took the ferry to the train station. Uldine was a dear baby, just quiet and content to nurse. Jim seemed content too, and played in the aisle with a rope secured around his waist.

The train ride took four hours, and a reminder of my journey just a few years before. A journey that began my life as it was now unfolding. I stepped off the train with the baby in my arms and Jim tethered at my side. I looked all around me. No one was there to greet me. I watched as the slow train chugged out of the station, leaving me bewildered and feeling abandoned.

I had no choice, so I headed up the rocky path to the road and headed in the direction of Eva's. I had never been to Heart's Delight, but Gordon assured me Eva would be there to greet me. She lived just a short walk from the train stop. I could see someone in the distance walking toward us. Here came Eva, who I only knew from pictures, but there was no trouble recognizing her. Braids rolled up on either side of her head and a determined walk, much as I had imagined her.

With open arms, she wrapped us all in hugs and kisses. She took Uldine from me and kissed her dear little face. Ambrose walked not far behind and he too hugged me.

"Untie the boy and I'll carry him. You must be tired, maid," he said.

"The kettle is on the stove, time's a wasting," interrupted Eva.

Jim did not kick or cry and I watched as he fell limp into Ambrose's outstretched arms.

So, this is the woman who saved my husband from the orphanage. I could see by her stern face and determined walk that she was the force behind her household. My visit lasted only the one night, but I was treated with kindness. Eva, curious, questioned why I would leave Gordon when I was about to have a child. I knew Gordon was her pride and joy so I stepped carefully and put all the blame on myself.

"Eva, Gordon is a wonderful husband and I miss him. It's just that I missed my family so much and I wanted them to see my babies. It's a great comfort to have my own mother deliver my little girl. I think you can understand that, having lost your mother when you were so young," I answered.

The next day we took the same journey back by train. I had not slept well for days and the birth and the travel were wearing on me. Father was at the ferry waiting for me the next evening and he carried Jim and all my bags. Mother had a late supper on the table ready.

There were biscuits and lamb stew and a blueberry pie. Mother placed a yellow flowered pot with strong tea on the table. I nursed while I ate, almost too tired to chew.

"I'll prepare hot water for a tub and then I will bathe the baby and Jim so you can get some rest. You're going to make yourself sick if you don't rest. You've got a long journey ahead, my girl. Gordon called while you were gone. It's time for you to return and be a family." She looked at me, closely gauging my reaction.

"Yes, Mother, of course, you're right and I'm ready to go home." I called Gordon myself that night and told him.

Gordon surprised me. "I'll pick you up in an automobile. I bought it for two hundred dollars. It's not too fancy, just an old Ford, but it runs."

I prayed to myself that going back was what I should do. Twillingate was home once, but I called America home now. I had been strong enough to leave once, and would be stronger now that I was going back to Gordon.

CHAPTER 24

MY RETURN

1930
GLADYS

The ship arrived in Sydney, Nova Scotia as scheduled. I gathered little Jim, rope around his waist, and the baby swaddled in my arms. A kind porter helped me carry my bags to the dock. I could see Gordon waving and walking fast towards us and then he ran.

He wrapped his arms around me with baby Uldine between us. He kissed me with such passion and tenderness. Then he kissed his new baby girl.

"She's beautiful, just like you," he said. There were tears in my eyes.

"Don't cry," he smiled. "We're going to be just fine. Don't worry, don't ever worry."

"I love you. I was afraid you might not come back."

I felt the tears well up in my eyes. Jim wrapped himself around his father's pant leg. Gordon swung him up in the air.

"Did you have a grand time with your Gramps, son?"

"No," Jim said. His new favorite word. "No" to everything.

We all hopped into the "new" car, a faded black Ford limousine. It could not have looked finer to me.

"We've got a lot of miles ahead of us. We could drive straight through if you're up to it."

"How long will that be?" I asked, weary from the journey. I was anxious for home but Jim and the baby would be restless and crying.

"It's about a twelve hour drive." Gordon looked at me cautiously for a reaction.

"We can stop for a bit and stretch our legs, a gas-up. There are cabins along the way if it's too much for you and the baby and Jim."

"Let's give it a go," I said, being as positive as I could. "If it's too much I'll let you know."

So off we went with the car sputtering from time to time. It put Jim and the baby to sleep. Thank God for that.

"I've so much to tell you about. The boys and I are going to start a business. You know Jerry King and Al Russell and my brother Bill." I nodded. "Well I have my eye on a truck, a stake body, and I can pay for it every month till it's mine. There is a fenced lot across from the Green Parrot for rent. I'll keep the truck there. I've been giving the boys rigging school at the Green Parrot. They don't know much but they're willing."

"I painted another steeple in East Cambridge for a Catholic church. Strangest thing, I saw a nun in the garden sitting on a bench crying. I asked her if she was ailin'."

"She said, 'No sir. I'm pregnant' and she cried some more."

"'Not the end of the world is it now?' I said."

"'It is for me,' she said."

"I went back to work but I wondered all day. 'How does a nun get pregnant?' I thought it must be a priest."

"Glad, am I boring you? Are you asleep?"

"No, no. Just thinking to myself how wonderful it is to hear you tell all your stories again."

I could hardly keep my eyes open but my mind wandered to what would be Gordon's motley crew. All Newfoundlanders. Al Russell was a small but pleasant man with a strange ailment that affected his fingernails - his nails were tiny stubs unlike nails at all. Jerry King always had an unlit cigar perched in the corner of his mouth. And then there was brother Bill with his unsmiling face and a wandering eyeball from a work-related accident.

What a crew!

CHAPTER 25

HOME AT LAST

1930
GLADYS

The apartment looked smaller than I remembered, but it was spotless and warm.

"Look in the bedroom, Glad." Gordon smiled as he led the way.

"Oh, bless Aunt Fannie. Uldine, you have a fine basinet to sleep in." I hugged her close and kissed her dear head. "Look, she bought nappies and nighties too."

Young Jim looked annoyed with all the attention the baby was getting, which was only natural.

"Jim boy, how do you like being home and with a baby sister no less?" his father asked.

"No," he said.

Of course he would say that, I thought. You could hardly blame him for being upset.

"Come now, we love you too. I'll get you something special for your homecoming. How's about that, son?"

Jim smiled and for once nodded "yes."

"We must plan a christening for all our family and friends for a celebration," I said excitedly.

"Wonderful idea, Glad. But if there's more little ones on the way, we'll need to find a larger apartment," said Gordon, looking at the spare bedroom.

Our second bedroom wasn't much larger than a closet. It would have to do for now. The baby would stay in our room and we would move Jim's crib to the small bedroom. I thought Jim might not like it, but we wouldn't get a minute's sleep if we were all in the same room.

Gordon and I planned the christening for the end of June at St. James's. Fannie and Heber would be Uldine's godparents. Sue and Frank were Jim's godparents. If Lucy had been nearer to us, I would have chosen her. I always hoped that we would all go to New York someday soon to visit. I missed Lucy terribly but I didn't want to bring it up with Gordon just yet.

"Here you go, Jim boy, just as I promised." Gordon had bought Jim a spinning top as he promised for a homecoming gift. Jim figured it out and had it spinning all over the hardwood floors, from one room to another. I felt content. Gordon seemed happy and loving. Jim, although still ill-tempered at times, could be happy making a bit of noise with the pots and pans or spinning his top across the wood floors.

Uldine was as I prayed for, quiet and content. As we cuddled in bed that first night, the children slept soundly but I just couldn't settle down, I tossed and turned. I ran over the day's events, all the excitement kept me awake. Gordon lay in bed reading the day's race results.

I turned to him and said, "Gordon, tell me another story please, something from when you were younger before we met." Gordon was happy to oblige when I asked, and I usually fell asleep in his arms listening to his adventures.

CHAPTER 26

GORDON TALKS

1923
GLADYS

"Sure thing, Glad. I'll be happy to tell you a story." Gordon got that gleam in his eye I knew so well. I finally felt warm as he pulled the covers up close around me. He began his story.

"It was about 1923, you see, before I met you. I was working in Canada. I had a couple of jobs there. One day a fellow asked me if I could run a crane because the operator was sick. I never saw a crane in my life! But I told him I could probably manage it. The boss told me I could try, and he showed me . . . more or less. I worked without mishap for a week, until the operator returned. I must have been about seventeen at the time and so I stayed there all winter until the next spring."

"Around that same time, my brother and another young man had left Canada, and landed in the United States. I decided to try and find them, and see if I could get some work with them. I found Bill and his friend living near Boston. I landed not far from him in Chelsea. There was a big mill in Chelsea at the time, Revere Rubber. I tried for a week, but failed to get a job, so I decided to sign up on a Japanese boat, an oil tanker. I was supposed to sail in the next day or two."

As Gordon told his story I imagined him on a large black vessel with red sails, cruising through exotic ports of call around Japan. Gordon resumed his narrative, I closed my eyes and visualized bowls of steaming rice and spices, served by Oriental ladies in scarlet kimonos, like the Thomas Cook posters I'd seen near Macy's. I was jolted out of my musings by Gordon's voice.

"When I got back to my boarding house that night, the

landlady told me I had a call from Mr. Russell from the Revere Rubber plant. He would like to see me first thing in the morning. I went to see Mr. Russell at the mill and he offered me a job. I forgot about the Japanese boat and glad that I did. They probably all spoke broken English, and I guess I never would have gotten along with all those men anyways. I worked along with Mr. Russell and he was very proud of me, if I do say so myself."

"I was very accurate and quick to learn. He'd show me something once and never had to show me again. I worked with him all summer, and I got my brother a job there too. When we were not working, we would all get together and talk. We would meet at Chelsea Square and go to the dances. We knew some young girls from Canada and Newfoundland. We would all go out together and dance. Nothing rough. We were just sociable fellows and never got into any trouble."

My sleepiness interrupted, I listened closely, feeling uncomfortable as he mentioned local girls from home and the dances down in Chelsea. I painfully remembered that Rita girl from the Green Parrot. But, as Gordon droned on, my eyes began getting heavy again.

CHAPTER 27

EXPLOSION!

1920s
GLADYS

"Did I ever tell you the time about the explosions?"

My eyes shot wide open and once again I was awake and hanging on his every word.

"No, no tell me," I encouraged him.

Gordon continued.

"After Revere Rubber, I worked for Beacon Oil, a refinery company in Everett, Massachusetts. During my time there we had three major explosions and one minor explosion. On the day of the minor explosion, I was working in the boiler shop changing some pumps. Luckily, there wasn't much damage from that explosion. But, the other three explosions caused a lot of damage, and a few fellows were killed. Some were hurt. I was fortunate each time because I had those days off."

"Normally I'm the man up in the air climbing around the steel where everything happens. During the last explosion, my foreman was standing by one of the gin poles that we used for joisting steel. We did everything by hand. We worked hard, plugged holes, small, large, and larger. They were heavy enough to lift to capacity. The foreman always asked me to check everything on top. That was my job. But at this explosion, the foreman was standing beside the pole we had set up before my day off. The engineer was sitting on the steam engine about 20-25 feet away from where the fire took place, and the explosion was so near the soaking drums that they blew up."

Gordon's eyes got watery and his voice broke as he continued his tale.

"The foreman burnt every bit of his clothes to his bare skin. The engineer was thrown and landed on a pile of steel and that was the end of him. Mr. Muckler, the foreman walked 300 or 400 feet till the ambulance came. I went to the hospital twice to visit him. He could only talk a little bit. The foreman's hands were burned and all the hair on his head and body. After two weeks of suffering he passed away."

Stunned by this story, all my sleepiness faded away as I thought how close I had come to never meeting Gordon.

CHAPTER 28

BY THE SEAT OF HIS PANTS

1920s
GLADYS

I sat up in bed as Gordon continued his narrative.

"As you can imagine I only worked at that place for about another week or two and I decided to look for another job. One of my buddies, Billie, told me he had a job for me."

"'What kind of job?' I asked. 'A job' he said. I didn't want to look a gift horse in the mouth so I agreed to go. Billie took me to meet the superintendent, a Mr. George, and then walked away. Mr. George asked me about my work experience and how long I had worked. I told him about all my jobs since I was twelve. I was about twenty-two years old at the time."

"'Well,' Mr. George said, 'Billie told me you could run this job and take care of the derricks.'"

"If there had been a hole in the floor, I would have gone straight through it! I was not wise to it - to take charge of a job - and I didn't know what to say. He asked me what I knew about blueprints."

"I wasn't a liar, so I said, 'You could fill a BIG book with what I don't know about blueprints. I know nothing!'"

"'Well, what you don't know I will show you,' he said."

"'If that's how you feel about it, I will do the best I can.'"

"So he took me to the job and he rolled out the blueprints to show me. They looked like a newspaper. I could read the writing, but didn't know about the drawings. He then introduced me to the engineers and showed me the two derricks."

"My job was to pick up the steel hook, climb on to pick up the steel, hook on to it, and send them on up in the air for the men to connect. The steel was simple because it all went by numbers. I would send up the steel and tell the boys to put a bolt in each end of it. Then I would get on top and help them connect the beams. I would climb up like a cat with a wrench in my hand and help the men tighten up the bolts and put rivets in. Every time, Mr. George would whistle and tell me to get down. I said, 'Sir, I can't sit on my fanny.'"

"So, he asked me if I could rivet. I said yes, so he sent me to the riveting crew. The job lasted three months. Then the brickwork started and most of the ironworkers were laid off."

I was sound asleep before he had finished his story.

CHAPTER 29

LOCKE STREET

1932
GLADYS

Our family was growing, and just as Gordon had predicted, we would soon need a larger home.

A few months after my return from Twillingate, Gordon and I found a three-bedroom apartment on the ground floor of a two-family home, an older brown clapboard house, and a far cry from the brownstones in Manhattan. However, the Locke Street apartment was spacious, and boasted a nice back and front porch.

The apartment was in walking distance to Davis Square. During the early 1900s, people chose to live around this area of Somerville where new homes and land were plentiful. The commute to downtown Boston for work was convenient and train connections were good.

Gordon's brother lived a few blocks away, not that we socialized that often, but still it was nice to know we had family nearby. St. James's Church was only a mile or two down Massachusetts Avenue. Best of all was Gordon's find, a chain-link fenced lot across the avenue, and it was for lease! Gordon intended to lease it for his new business.

"I think I can buy a Diamond Reo for a fair price," he told me. "It may take a bit to save the money but this is the start of our dreams, Glad. Our own business!" Gordon beamed and I smiled too, happy as a fool.

"I don't even know what a Diamond Reo is, but if it makes you this happy, it must be good." I gave him a long kiss for good luck, our good luck.

"It's a big truck, just what we need to haul heavy equipment. Can't you see it?"

"G.H. Harnum Rigging & Trucking. Glad, it's all gonna happen!"

I hadn't told him yet but we were going to need all the blessings from family, friends, and the Good Lord, because, yes . . . another little Harnum was on the way.

"I've learned enough from every job before to run a business with honest hard work. I told you everything would be fine, and it is." He grabbed me around the waist and we did a do-si-do all around the kitchen table. The bright red and white checks of the tablecloth seemed to spin around in a whirr.

But it wasn't that easy in the end. It would take many months of standing in line for work until Gordon could get enough money together to pay for the truck and lease the lot across the avenue.

In the meantime, Fannie and Heber were doing well, but they still had no children. I felt sorry for them. I knew they would make wonderful parents. By this time, Sue and Frank had a daughter, little Audrey. Sue confided in me and said there would only be one. I knew why, as I remembered our talk on my wedding day and her dislike of her "duty" as a wife. In January 1932 I gave birth to my third child, another bundle of joy, Edna Louise Harnum. She took after her father and was a bright and curious baby.

CHAPTER 30

CHRISTMAS EVE

1932
GORDON

It had been another hard winter, but as usual I was up before dawn and this Christmas Eve morning was no different. Gladys watched me from underneath the blankets as I put on multiple layers of clothing, and topped it off with my old grey tweed coat, and a muffler wrapped around my face and neck. Gladys kissed me goodbye, and she waved out the window as I walked towards Somerville Avenue.

It was frigid walking down Somerville Avenue. I stuck my hands deeper into the pockets of my wool coat, and continued down Porter Square. I turned onto Union Square in Cambridge. The weather was atrocious, but I perked myself up by humming a little tune and walked through Charlestown to Sullivan Square. It was a long walk and I still had to hike over the bridge into Boston, then over to Atlantic Avenue. I quickened my pace so I wouldn't miss the ferry to East Boston.

Atlantic Avenue had an elevated loop with a stop at Rowe's Wharf. The stairwell was visible in front of the building. A line of passengers clambered to get on the ferry to East Boston. The cost was three cents. By daybreak I was at the East Boston Labor Exchange waiting in line for work.

"Hey you! Yeah, in the gray coat. Are you ready to work?"

I jumped at the opportunity and got a day's work. All day long, I carried fifty-pound bags of coal up three flights of stairs to "three-deckers" in East Boston. At the end of the day I was leg-sore and weary, but a happy man. I clutched eight dollars in my fist.

Darkness descended by the time I took the ferry back to Boston. The chill bit into me as I made my way over the bridge to Charlestown. I retraced my morning's steps through Sullivan Square and Somerville to Porter Square. I reached Porter Square late but the stores were still open for last-minute Christmas shoppers. I pulled out the handful of crumpled dollar bills. With my last dollars I bought presents for Gladys and the children. I still had enough left over to buy a small Christmas tree.

And so, I returned home to my family on Locke Street.

I knew that Gladys would be fretting. I heard an audible sigh when she heard the comforting sound of the key in the front door. As she jumped up to meet me at the door, I hugged her. My hands were full of presents and a Christmas tree. The children wrapped themselves around my legs.

I looked into Gladys's eyes and caught my breath, as I realized what a lucky man I was.

Gladys stood there with tears running down her face and said, "Oh, Gordon, thank you so much. I love you."

CHAPTER 31

DIAMOND REO

1933
GLADYS

Spring was in the air, and I sat on the edge of the bed day-dreaming. I watched as the robins pecked over the grass in the backyard. It was way past the "early bird catches the worm" time. Time to get up and going. Winter had been long this year, and the snow had been too deep to push the baby pram. Eager to be outside, I asked Jim if he would like to go for a walk with his sisters to the square.

"Let's pick up your wooden blocks off the kitchen floor and put them away, eh Jim, then we'll get the girls dressed."

"Why?" He gave me a sulky look.

"Because, I need to get a few things to make supper, the sun is out, and it's a lovely day." I smiled, hoping he would agree and not give me an argument again.

"Be a good boy and get ready. I'll gather your sisters and off we'll go."

Oh, thank goodness for my sweet girls, I thought.

Uldine was already putting on her jacket. Louise and Uldine were ready and eager for a little sunshine too.

"Let's go out and get some fresh air. Uldine, you get to ride in the carriage."

"Cawwidge." She smiled at me and my heart skipped a bit. Did she really try to say carriage? I lifted her from the crib and she smiled again. Such a pleasant child I thought to myself.

"Louise, you need a fresh nappy, then in the bunting you go."

She cooed and tried to suck on her hand. I nursed her just a

75

bit so she would be content on our walk.

Jim walked along holding onto the rope tied to the carriage. There was still a chill in the air, but the sun felt warm on my back as we walked over to Davis Square. First stop the A&P; they were the largest grocers in the area. I needed vegetables for tonight's soup and maybe a whole chicken. The square was busy with shoppers, the energy and hustle-bustle made me feel renewed.

The weather had brought the housewives out of hibernation, like the groundhog out of his hole. On the way to the market, some outdoor stalls had been set up. They were filled with the colors of early spring produce, canned food items, and a few hanging butchered meats.

Jim eyed a glass jar at the register with red, white, and blue swirly suckers. "Jim, would you like a sucker?" I asked, knowing the response.

"A red one," he replied.

"What do we say?"

He thought for a moment. "Please."

The cashier handed him a large red sucker.

"What do we say?"

He mumbled, "Thank you," as the sucker popped into his mouth. At least he would be happy on the walk home.

Gordon had said he would be home early. He hoped to make a deal with the owner of a Diamond Reo, a special truck he wanted to buy. I had dinner ready and waiting, and made something special: tapioca for dessert - Gordon's favorite and easy to feed to children.

I passed my neighbor's house as we walked down the sidewalk. We waved and said hello. It was a short walk back, and as I took a deep breath the aroma of spring assailed my nostrils. Soon, the trees would be in bloom and the daffodils would poke their sleepy heads through the earth.

A few minutes later we arrived home. "Jim, let's get washed up for dinner," I instructed him. I fed and washed the girls and started dinner. I set Uldine down in the playpen, with clothespins to play with. Louise, no one ever called her Edna, went down for a nap in her bassinet.

As I finished the final touches on our meal, I heard the heavy front door open and shut. Gordon. I listened as he scuffed the dirt off his shoes on the rug.

"How's my boy?" he asked Jim, who had found his blocks and was stacking them on the floor.

"I got a sucker." He looked up and smiled at his father.

"Were you a good soldier boy today?"

"I'm NOT a soldier," he corrected.

"I know, I know. Good boy." Jim nodded.

"What's for dinner, Glad?" We hugged and I adjusted my apron and turned back to stirring the pot of pea soup.

"Pea soup and a chicken in the oven. Tapioca for dessert."

"Exactly what I wanted," and he chuckled.

He never laughed out loud till the end, and then he whooped as if he were gasping for breath. It always made me smile.

"The Boston Herald is on the table."

Gordon washed up at the kitchen sink and sat down to read the paper. I set the dishes on the table, careful not to spill any as I set the soup bowls down. I only had two tablecloths. Both were from Fannie, and this one, the red plaid, was my favorite.

I set the whole roast chicken on a platter for Gordon to carve. I inhaled as the aroma snaked around the table, my mouth watering.

"Jim, get your pillow and set it in your chair. Time to eat."

Jim climbed up with his pillow and I straightened it out so he sat high enough to reach the table.

"Let's say Grace."

Jim folded his hands like we did.

"God is good, God is great, and we thank him for our food which we are about to receive. Amen."

Jim said the "Amen" extra loud.

"So how was work today?" I asked Gordon.

"Well, I met with Mr. Murphy who owns the Diamond Reo. He's over near Heber's by Inman Square. He's willing to sell the Reo and take payments. Looks to be in good shape too, but I'm no mechanic. I'll ask Heber to take a look at it first, before I make the deal. He knows more about mechanics than I do. It's a flatbed, called a straight job, White Motor Company, just what we need to haul tanks."

"I'm going to work any other job that I can get, until we start making money anyways. Heber offered me money to get started but I like to do things on my own. He never took any money for his old Ford and I appreciated that, but you know, I don't like to borrow anything."

I nodded and picked Uldine up from the playpen. I spooned pea soup into her mouth. She was hungry after our outing in the fresh air and slurped her soup. I wiped her face on her bib.

"Tapioca for dessert." We all liked tapioca.

I scooped out small dishes of it.

"Ummm, good, right?" I said as I spooned a mouthful into Uldine.

Jim spilled a little then licked what he spilt off the tablecloth.

"Don't do that, son!" from his father.

Jim looked sheepish, but stopped. I got a wet rag and wiped the tapioca off my favorite tablecloth. I cleared the table, and got the children ready for bed.

Jim had a tiny cot in the corner of the children's bedroom. We said our prayers, and I tucked everyone into bed.

Gordon relaxed and, sitting in the living room, listened to

the news on the radio. I finished up in the kitchen, wiped my hands on my apron, and hung it over the kitchen chair.

Our favorite together time was when we were both pulled up next to the radio. Sometimes we listened to Charlie Chan. (In later years, we would listen to the Green Hornet. We would sit side by side in anticipation, wondering whom the Green Hornet would save from the bad guys that night.)

Of course, the news was a priority for Gordon, but luckily nothing of great interest happened today, a nice ending to a long day.

CHAPTER 32

A VISIT FROM COUSIN WILF

1932
GLADYS

I think back on those times and wonder how Gordon was able to support all of us.

Then one day we had a visit from my cousin Wilf from Newfoundland. Cousin Wilf was a clever man with a good sense of humor. Tall, with glasses and graying hair, he had kind blue eyes. He liked to travel and this was his first visit to us.

He and Gordon were getting along so well, that after dinner I said, "Why don't you tell cousin Wilf one of your stories."

Cousin Wilf, being no stranger to a good Newfie story, encouraged him.

"Well, well, Wilf," he said, and I could see him warming up to the "task" of storytelling.

"Ya see, I got a good job at Pappas Construction. We only had two children at the time, and the boss made me a rigging foreman. The job was wrapping up; I had been there about a year, doing form steel work for them."

"There were these cranes along the railroad. Mobile cranes, two large cranes called locomotive cranes, a 17 and a 90. You know what they are, Wilf?" Wilf nodded. "Well the 90 was a bog train. Anytime you wanted to move it out, the railroad ties were put down. So this day I was moving some steel and I signaled to the operator to put the steel in a certain spot. I was standing on the steel, and the men were just outside."

"Mr. Ackerman, the superintendent of Pappas Construction,

didn't want the steel where I had signaled the engineer to put it. The engineer was watching him, and instead he swung the crane and steel, and dropped it on my foot and leg."

A shiver went up my spine as I thought of it all over again, especially the hard times we had afterward.

"So it rolled over my foot, yup, five tons of steel, and onto one of my legs, caught the foot and ankle but I was protected by a steel angle. The angle saved me from having my foot cut off. I yelled for the engineer to pick the steel up. Mr. Ackerman ran over to apologize."

"They called the ambulance and put me on a stretcher and took me to first aid. Every bone in my foot and ankle were broken. They operated on me the next day and set the ankle. My foot was twisted into an awkward angle. They had to push it up an inch and a half for my foot to be somewhat normal."

"I was out of hospital on the fourth week, and back to driving on the fifth week."

"I had Heber's old Ford back then, a soft top with ridges. I tied the crutches up on the roof when I was driving. I drove the car with one foot, ya see."

"So, one night the police stopped me. They wanted to know what the crutches were for. I told them what the problem was with my leg."

"'Leg in a cast,' I said, 'the leg is broken.'"

"'How do you drive?' one of the policemen asked."

"I said, 'Easy, I go from the gas to the brake and clutch all at the same time.' The copper shook his head, and said nothing. But he let me go. Ha!"

CHAPTER 33

RIGGING SCHOOL
AT THE GREEN PARROT

1933
GLADYS

"Well boys, we are now officially a rigging team," Gordon puffed out his chest. "We have the right truck and we already have our first job."

A group of men were gathered around listening to Gordon. They were at the smoky bar of the Green Parrot Pub having a quick nip.

"Now, you all know how to tie knots, rigging knots. First, we're gonna piece the tanks together with rivets. Load them onto the truck and assemble them at the site. I'll shimmy up the side and rivet the top. Simple."

Gordon took quick stock of his men. They were all hard workers but Gordon had asked them to try something different. I knew how important this meeting was to him.

"I don't know, Gordon, this is all new to me," said Al, shaking his head, uncertain they could pull it off.

"I've done it all before. I'll teach you as we go, Al." He beamed a big smile.

Jerry adjusted the cigar in his mouth and cleared his throat, "Well, boy, if you say we can, I guess we can."

Al was a runt of a man with stubby chewed up fingernails. He needed the work and the money. He knew Gordon was ambitious and experienced. Just what the men needed to make a go of it and put some cash in their pockets.

Brother Bill didn't say much. His one lazy eye strayed out of focus as he looked around the room. You could never be sure if he was looking straight at you or not.

Bill chimed in. "My brother will make it happen. I'll give him that much."

"Let's raise a glass to that," said the bartender, who had been leaning in on their conversation.

"First drink is on the house!"

The Diamond Reo was old but it ran well. It sat safely behind a chain-link fence just across Massachusetts Avenue in clear sight of the Green Parrot. It wasn't likely to get stolen either. Gordon put a giant padlock on the gate to secure it.

The next day, the ropes and blocking were loaded into the old Ford that now served as a pick-up. The first job was in East Boston. The men riveted and assembled the tanks. Then they raised them up thirty to forty feet by climbing up the sides with ropes and a bosun's chair.

I handled all the billing and accounting for G. H. Harnum Rigging & Trucking. I wrote checks for all the men who worked for us.

We were raised to be workers, not complainers. We were grateful for all our blessings.

CHAPTER 34

EIGHT CHETWYND ROAD

1930s
GLADYS

In 1933 G.H. Harnum Rigging & Trucking was founded on a dream. The following year, my second son Gordon Lester was born. That made four. He was a handsome boy, with blond hair and crystal blue eyes, like his father's.

On Sundays we walked or drove to St. James's Church. The children wore the best clothes we could afford. Most of them were hand-me-downs, but they were always scrubbed and ironed. I wanted us to look our best as a family.

Sometimes Gordon attended church, and other times he would go out on scouting jobs. No matter what, we always had Sunday dinner together. We had what I hoped was a typical prosperous middleclass life.

Our friends Laura and Les occasionally came over on a Saturday evening. We'd play Canasta, Rummy, or Hearts. Laura took cards very seriously, and chastised Les if he didn't play his hand well. Les always agreed and always apologized.

Gordon liked to tease her a bit.

"It's only a game, Laura," he would say.

She would look at him, but wouldn't crack a smile. When she played, she played to win.

I put the children to bed when we had company. Laura was always amazed that with four children, my house was always immaculate.

She would say, "You never smell a drop of pee at Gladys's house." I smiled, but inwardly cringed.

Laura was from a family of thirteen and never wanted

children. Maybe her poor mother couldn't keep up with all the housework and the smell of pee. Maybe Laura got tired of changing her younger siblings' diapers.

Our family of nieces and nephews was on the rise. Sue and Frank had a daughter, Audrey. Lucy and Steve had four youngsters. Fannie and Heber still had no children.

The business thrived and so did our family. We rented a small cape on Chetwynd Road in North Cambridge. A year later in 1935 our daughter Dorothy Eunice was born.

My dear mother passed away from pneumonia in 1936. At the time I had a newborn and four children to care for. It was a sad time, made sadder because I was not able to attend her funeral or return home to console my poor father.

In 1937 we had another son, William Frank, who we called Bill. But in 1937 I hit a bump in our idyllic life. I had a difficult delivery with Bill, and it left me paralyzed on my left side. The doctors thought I might never use my left arm again. I was upset with the prognosis, but I was not about to give up. I forced my arm to pin up clothes on the clothesline, and what-ever else I needed two arms for, I forced myself to do it. In time, my arm worked just fine.

By the late 1930s we had enough in the bank to buy 8 Chetwynd Road. It was our first home. Chetwynd Road had eight identical shingled Cape Cod homes, four on each side of the road. The street dead-ended at a four-foot cement retaining wall with a ten-foot, chain-link fence. The fence enclosed Raymond Park.

The house was a great find, and the park had a jungle gym and swings. In the winter the city would flood a part of the park and the neighborhood kids learned to ice skate. The kids would pull the chain-link fence out just enough to slide under and crawl into the park. It was quicker than walking around to the Upland Road entrance. Sometimes I'd catch our boys climbing the fence, just to show off. If it snowed, the kids would take cardboard and slide down the icy hills in the park. It was a nice area for our children to grow up in.

Number 8 had two bedrooms and a bathroom upstairs. The downstairs had a living room, dining room, and kitchen. We had a nice enclosed front porch. Off the kitchen was a back hall with the refrigerator. The house was a tight fourteen hundred square feet. There was a gas log in the living room, and radiators in every room that knocked and hissed steam in the winter. Wet mittens and socks went on the radiators in winter to dry. I have fond memories of those years.

The garbage man came once a week to pick up our trash. He would drop the food scraps into the dump truck to feed his pigs. The Hood Milk man also came once a week with a metal-handled carrier that held six quart glass bottles. I loved to see the cream floating at the top of the bottle. It brought back fond memories of my Twillingate home in Newfoundland and our cream-loving cats.

The Happy Home Bakery delivered our bread and baked goods. The deliveryman's name was Red - Red the Baker - and yes, we teased him because he had red hair.

The ragman came around once in a while in his old jalopy. He gathered old clothes and rags and sold them by the pound.

Since space was tight, Gordon and I turned the dining room into our bedroom. The girls slept in one of the upstairs bedrooms and the boys in the other one. Everyone got a bath in the porcelain tub on Saturday nights. Girls bathed first, all in the tub at once. Then we would re-fill it for the boys. But our carefree days at Number 8 were to change over the course of the next few years.

1940s

CHAPTER 35

RATIONING

1940
GORDON

We knew that Great Britain was entering the war. Once again we feared the start of another depression. After World War II began, the first commodity to be controlled was petrol. By January 1940 bacon, butter, and sugar rationing began. These were followed by successive ration schemes for meat, tea, jam, biscuits, eggs, milk, and tinned fruit. We were issued ration cards. We received primarily butter and sugar, but gas was the most important item for the company. We were rationed although America would not actually enter the war until 1941. Our top priority for now was petrol for the trucks so we could continue to work.

The business was going well, but we had a lot of gas-hungry vehicles to feed. There were two stake body trucks or panel trucks as we called them. Also, a GMC pick-up and a storage unit for the ropes and block-and-tackle we used, plus all the tools at the lot on Massachusetts Avenue.

The business included jobs moving machinery in and out of factories like Deran's Confectionery and Nabisco. My sister-in-law Sue worked for Nabisco on the assembly line then. She told us that sometimes the pigeons flew in through the roof vents and fell into the batter and no one did anything about it.

Gladys wouldn't buy Nabisco crackers after she heard that. It's a wonder that she ate Jello after I told her they used horse hooves and bones to make it. We heard all the bad details of what went on in the factories that made our food. Our men saw all of this while they were moving the machinery in and out.

CHAPTER 36

ALL IN THE FAMILY

1940s
GLADYS

During these years my daughters Uldine and Louise were inseparable. They played quietly together. On the other hand Dorothy, or Dot as we liked to call her, was a tomboy and quick to tell her brothers off. She usually had scraped knees and scuffed brown oxfords from running through the neighborhood, her long braids flying in the wind. My other girls were more lady-like.

One time when Dot was about three, she came running into the house so proud and excited. "Ma, Ma! A man backed into me with his car and gave me a nickel." She gave me a big grin.

Thank God she wasn't hurt! She was too pleased with earning a nickel to realize the danger she had been in.

The boys were very different. Jim liked to aggravate his sisters and sometimes got in brawls with his brother Gordon. Bill was much younger, and was often on his own much like his sister Dot.

Although gasoline was in short supply, Gordon knew how to combine work with pleasure. One weekend Gordon suggested we take a road trip. Everyone jumped at the chance to spend time with Dad. They all wanted to go for a ride, including me. Gordon's "rides" could go anywhere. A ride was sometimes just a trip to a parking lot behind a factory. We played in the lot while he walked around and estimated a job. It was worth it just to spend time with him.

On rare occasions we packed a lunch and drove to Revere Beach on the North Shore. We didn't wear bathing suits. We didn't own any because none of us knew how to swim. The children were only allowed to step into the edge of the water. Revere Beach was alive with sidewalk vendors selling root beer and lemon-aide, peanuts and popcorn. We always had a good time, and the war seemed a long way away.

CHAPTER 37

WORLD WAR II

1939-1945
GLADYS

Although we knew it was coming, the news of another world war was horrific. Along with rationing, Gordon and I read the papers, listened to the radio, or watched the newsreels at our local cinema. Even before the unimaginable details of the war were made public, we listened to the few details that weren't censored. Blackouts, planes dropping bombs, while bomb shelters were filled to capacity. The loss of our Allied soldiers was devastating.

How unaware and naïve we were in our little corner of Cambridge paradise, so well insulated from the genocide and horrors going on in Europe. Three times a day, the national news came on with updates. Gordon and I huddled around the radio to listen when we could. We learned little, government control and censorship of the news was comprehensive.

As time passed we heard the real horror stories. Millions of Jews were sent to the gas chambers. Barbaric research was going on in Germany, including the torture of adults, sympathizers, children, and the elderly, all considered unworthy to live in the eyes of the Nazis.

I think back on those years and wonder how so much evil went on while our lives were virtually unchanged at 8 Chetwynd Road. Life continued on in the Harnum family. I had my hands full raising six children. We ate what we could get, slept, and worked hard, almost oblivious to the tragedy in Europe until it was our turn.

On September 1, 1939 as Hitler invaded Poland, my children invaded the halls of Peabody Elementary School. The children walked the long mile over the hill to the school on Linnaean Street.

I gave them each a hug, and a lunch bag with peanut butter and jelly. If we had bologna, the boys wanted that instead. I put it on white Sunbeam bread. Gordon Jr. loved mayonnaise sandwiches. Just mayonnaise, ugh!

The school provided a half-pint bottle of milk to each child for free. I attended all the school conferences. Gordon could never seem to find the time. Really, I think he just found them awkward, having only finished third grade himself.

Church was a way to socialize as well as to find God. The children went to Sunday school and we saw my sister Sue most weekends. Gordon had a marvelous singing voice, and all the children would chime in loudly when he sang the hymns. I couldn't sing a note, but I was proud of all of them.

What I could do well was organize. I organized dinners and rummage sales to raise money for the church. Even with six children, I could find the time. I enjoyed organizing, and a church dinner for a hundred was not a challenge for me, it was a passion!

While overseas children were massively affected by the war, I tried to keep my own rag-tag army safe. One day the local photography studio advertised a package offer. The studio was just a block down from St. James's Church. My sister Sue and I both wanted professional portraits of our children. The special offer was five portraits for one price. I had six children and Sue had Audrey. We decided on one picture of Jim, one of Uldine and Louise together, Dorothy, Bill, and then another photo for Audrey.

The photographer offered to do a free photograph of young Gordon on the condition I would bring him back for a separate sitting. The photographer told us the photos would be used for advertising. Gordon, like his father, was a handsome blonde-haired, blue-eyed boy with pleasing features.

We returned to the studio the following week. At the second sitting, the photographer insisted that Sue and I wait outside. We went out to the waiting area and sat on the bench chatting so we wouldn't distract them.

Time passed as we sat in the hallway and we wondered why it was taking so long. I looked at Sue and she looked at me. We both decided something wasn't right. Call it mother's intuition if you will. I pounded on the door saying we needed to leave right away. Even then it took the photographer several minutes before he came to the door. We gathered Gordon and left immediately. We never went back.

That night when I put Gordon to bed I hugged him and asked him if anything was bothering him. I was fairly satisfied that nothing inappropriate had happened, but I knew little about those behaviors. I didn't tell his father, but my better instinct left a nagging doubt in my mind, which I never quite got over. As usual I read my Bible that night before turning in, grateful that nothing worse happened. I prayed for my husband and all the children.

CHAPTER 38

THE HUMAN FLY

1940s
GLADYS

We were blessed that Gordon had talent and an ability to find work, especially during the hard times when there was little work or food available. I called Gordon "The Human Fly." He scaled heights and painted flagpoles, hung off the side of bridges and painted them too. It seemed nothing was too tall for him. A shiver went up my spine as I imagined him swinging on a beam to set it in place while hanging hundreds of feet in the air.

His crews were not always willing to follow his daring lead. It took a special type of person to climb. If any of the men were fearful of heights, Gordon would ascend together by tying himself to the other man. Rigging required scrambling over machines and up radio towers. They went in and out of buildings several stories high to hoist machines into factories. Whatever the challenge, he always made it work.

I was in awe at his fearlessness. I was strong in faith, but not that type of brave. We had six children, and so I always prayed for his safe return home at night. One evening after dinner we were listening to the news. I commented on how dangerous the world was.

Gordon responded, "You worry too much, Glad."

"You nearly lost your leg in the last accident," I said. "You really should have sued them. I know they paid all your medical bills, but you still have bone splinters coming through your skin and catching on your socks."

"The doctor said that was a good thing, Gladys. If the bone splinters find a way out through my skin, then they won't travel to my heart and kill me."

"Some consolation!" I chastised him.

"With six hungry mouths to feed, those factory owners can afford to give you a settlement. Don't be too proud to accept what's due you."

"Glad, it's just a little limp. I'm just grateful that I'm healing. I've been promised work in the future from those very same factories."

"Oh, hogwash." I was angry. "As tough as you are, all they have to say is, 'Good job, Gordon,' and they can pull the wool right over your eyes in a second."

Putnam Avenue, Cambridge

Gordon's business was doing well despite my nagging and wartime shortages. One day he told me he had found an acre of land with a small brown-shingled home on the corner of Putnam Avenue. It was up for sale. It had been abandoned a while and he told me it needed work.

The property was not far from the Charles River on the one side and Central Square on the other side. We went to see it. A row of two and three family homes lined the streets, but it was also a mix of commercial and industrial properties.

"Gladys, factories that we've done many jobs for in the past are just a few blocks away." I recognized the glint of excitement in his eyes as I nodded.

"Deran's Confectionery and Nabisco are near here too. If I can get it for a fair price it would be perfect for the business!"

That wasn't to be the last we heard of Putnam Avenue.

CHAPTER 39

NEW YORK CITY

1940s
GLADYS

It was years since I'd seen my other sister Lucy. She lived in the Bronx with her husband and five children. I missed her terribly and always bemoaned that fact. Not long after that, Gordon got a work estimate job in New York City. He surprised us with an overnight family trip, including a visit with Lucy and her family. I called Lucy right away with the good news. I felt so excited I couldn't wait.

The children were excited, too, when I told them the news. I almost cried, I was so happy. We loaded into the old Ford. It was a tight squeeze, so we brought only one suitcase for all of us. That allowed us one change of clothes apiece. It was summer, but we all had sweaters if the night got chilly.

Lucy lived in the Bronx in a run down six-family home. As we drove up, trashcans lined the street ready for pick-up. It was a hot day and the city smelled dirty and the air felt heavy with humidity. We pulled up in front of a small chain-link fence. Their front yard had no grass, flowers, or bushes. The noise was deafening. Cars honked and trucks roared by, the air thick with exhaust fumes.

The children, oblivious to their surroundings, ran up the front steps and rang the bell. I hugged Lucy tightly to me and shook her husband Steve's hand. Gordon and my six young'uns were all smiles. Gordon shook Steve's hand.

"Glad to meet you, Steve," he said.

He gave Lucy a big hug, and she looked back nervously at her husband. Steve didn't like that. I could tell by the look on his face. Lucy had mentioned in her letters to me that Steve was unreasonably jealous.

She even wrote once to say that on a rainy day while walking back from her job at the hospital, a male co-worker drove by and offered her a ride home. When Steve found out, he was furious. He actually went to the hospital and made a scene.

"No men are to pick up my wife," he told the staff nurse.

I hugged Lucy and noticed how thin and tired she looked. Their five children looked much like mine. You could tell we were related.

Almost as soon as we arrived on the doorstep, my daughter Dot rushed in to use the bathroom. We were hardly inside the door before we heard a shout. A giant cockroach had greeted her on the bathroom wall. She came running out screaming bloody murder. She'd never seen a cockroach before. Lucy's children giggled. June, the oldest girl, looked down at Dot and said, "You've never seen a cockroach?"

Dot looked up at her with a brazen face. "We don't have 'kaka-roaches' where we're from!"

Leave it to Dot!

CHAPTER 40

CAMBRIDGE

1940-50s
GLADYS

As the years went flying by I felt the loss of my own Twillingate childhood. My two oldest boys Jim and Gordon were now in high school at Rindge Technical in Cambridge. It was just across a patch of grass from Cambridge High and Latin where Uldine, Louise, and Dot attended.

In those days the student population in the two high schools was about 2,000 and was quite diversified. Harvard University was a short walk away, and Harvard Square was always a cultural experience. People from all walks of life passed through the kiosk, located smack in the middle of the square. Newspapers and magazines from every part of the world were available there.

The Harvard Coop sat opposite the kiosk, bustling with students buying books and supplies. We could ride the trolley around town or take the underground straight into Boston. My five children walked the three miles to the Square; they would cut through Harvard Yard.

The Charles River separated Cambridge from Boston. In winter it was iced over but as soon as the ice broke, university crew teams rowed their slim boats at record pace, cutting through the dark polluted river. The Cambridge Sailing Club filled the river with small white sails fluttering in the wind. On the weekends and during regatta days, the banks were loaded with picnic baskets, blankets, scooters, and bicycles. We sat and people-watched as casual walkers promenaded on the sidewalk.

CHAPTER 41

"THE SHOP"

1940-50s
GLADYS

We were now proud owners of Putnam Avenue, lovingly referred to as "The Shop." I was the bookkeeper and accountant until now, a job I loved. Gordon wanted a fancy trained secretary and reluctantly I gave the reins over to our new employee Loretta. A buxom redhead, I took an instant distrust to her. She was from Newfoundland, not that being from Newfoundland made her less trustworthy. She looked a bit rough around the edges as far as I was concerned. Maybe she wore too much makeup, and talked unlike a lady. Maybe I was remembering Gordon's deception with Rita the redhead. I might be jealous, but I wasn't. Not really.

"The Shop" was filled with the smells of a garage - grease, dirt, machinery oils, and soiled uniforms. Two old wooden desks were covered with all the paraphernalia of a working office. File boxes, staples, rubber thumbs, elastic bands, and paper clips cluttered the tops. A typewriter, adding machine, check writer, and telephone sat on each desk waiting for business. The building included a modest half bathroom. The walls were covered in cheap dark paneling. There were two additional rooms, one for Gordon's office and the other a place for the men to change from street clothes to their grease-stained uniforms and coveralls. The spartan basement had a bathroom and shower. It was a place to work, with little warmth or decor.

We had plenty of work and enough money to buy a Mack truck. The Mack was dark green with a silver bulldog on the hood. It was my favorite part of the truck. We had enough extra for a Studebaker pickup, not new but serviceable and it was also painted in the same dark hunter green, and became the color for all the G. H. Harnum vehicles.

The only out-of-the ordinary employee was Squeaky the cat. Hired to keep the mouse and rat population to a minimum, Squeaky was a calico, what Gordon called a "money cat." The aroma of fishy cat food usually lingered in the air. Tabby Cat Food, one of our regular customers, donated cases for Squeaky.

CHAPTER 42

ROMANCE IS IN THE AIR

1940s
GLADYS

The girls were growing up quickly. Uldine fancied a fellow named Howard Walker. They met at St. James's. Howie was an imposing large man with dark almost black hair. He had a voice that was deep and commanding. He had only one arm, the other had been cut off just above the elbow. When he was about twelve years old, running and jumping from the rooftops with some other young boys, he fell and broke his arm. After they put his arm in a cast he developed blood poisoning and the arm had to be removed.

He seemed the total opposite of Uldine, my frail pretty girl, so soft-spoken and obedient. I worried and hoped that Howie would be the right choice for her. I heard them talking about marriage; she was only sixteen. Uldine was responsible and had an afterschool job at the New England Telephone Company. But like most sixteen-year-old girls, she seemed to dream only of marriage and children. If she only knew how hard it could be! I didn't want to spoil her dream.

Louise also had a male friend named Fred. He was a real character. They met at a Rindge Tech concert she and her friend Sheilagh were attending. Fred was sitting in the folding chair behind Louise and Sheilagh. He kicked Louise's chair, so he had an excuse to apologize and meet her. Louise was my tallest daughter at five feet, eight inches. She was a chubby girl but pretty, with big blue eyes and long wavy blond hair.

Fred was a year older and came from East Cambridge. A Polish boy, his family was first generation immigrants from Poland. They had a bakery business and a bar in East Cambridge. Fred pursued Louise for several years, and eventually got lucky. The very first time he came to visit us he wore a rope for a belt. Not so uncommon in those days. Dot could not hold back her remarks to Louise.

"Where did you find him? Under a rock!"

Dot was a good kid, even though she could be outspoken - a tomboy, always happier outdoors running than walking.

My younger son Gordon was a great student; he had already skipped one grade. He had young ladies clambering around him for attention.

His brother Bill had a pet white rat, and if it had been up to me, I wouldn't have allowed it. Gordon was okay with it, as long as he kept it in the cage on the porch.

I sat home one evening knitting, and wondered idly who would be the first to leave the nest.

It turned out to be a big shock!

CHAPTER 43

JIM TAKES A JOYRIDE

1940s
GLADYS

The phone rang and it was the police station asking for Gordon.

"What's happened? Has there been an accident?"

"No, no one is hurt, Mrs. Harnum, but we have your son, Neil James, in custody."

I felt weak and my knees started to buckle, "Jim! Oh, my God. Why?"

"Please ask your husband to come down to the station and we will discuss it."

"Did he do something?" I asked.

"Yes. He has been accused of stealing a car."

"Why?"

"I don't know why, Mrs. Harnum. Please, just ask your husband to come down to the Cambridge Precinct in Central Square."

I hung up the phone and immediately picked it back up and started dialing the shop. I asked for Gordon. Loretta, who was probably filing her fingernails, said he was out on a job.

"As soon as he returns . . . it's an emergency, could you send one of the men after him?"

"Is everything alright, Gladys?"

No, Loretta, it's not! "Just find him," I snapped.

The front door banged. Gordon rushed in. "Do you want to go get him with me?"

"Of course I do." I slammed down the phone and tore off my apron, grabbed my purse, and we jumped in the car.

There was silence for the first couple of miles, just the hiss of cars passing. Then Gordon started in.

"Why the hell would he steal a car?" Gordon ranted, then banged his hands on the steering wheel so hard my heart jumped with it. I waited in the car while he went into the police station. I could only hope that Gordon would post the bail without any altercation and bring Jim straight to the car.

Jim sauntered out of the precinct. He had on his favorite blue jeans and a white short-sleeve tee shirt with a pack of Lucky Strikes rolled up in the sleeve. I could swear there was a smirk on his face. Gordon was furious, his face turned dark, a flushed plum color.

"Get in the damn car," he shouted at Jim. Jim jumped in the back seat.

I pleaded with Gordon, my nerves on edge. "Don't say anything now while we're driving, or we'll end up in a car accident."

But when we got to the house all hell broke loose.

"This will be in the Boston Herald! Are you happy now?" he yelled into Jim's face. He was so upset, he was spitting. His face turned beet red, his eyes black with fury.

Jim stood there and said not a word. No apology, no remorse. It stunned me.

"Stop, stop this. It won't do any good now. It's done."

"You always defend him, always have. He's no damn good! Ungrateful pup," said his dad. Gordon rolled up his sleeves, which I knew meant trouble.

Before it could go any further or turn into a fistfight, I turned to Jim.

"Go to the back porch. Now! Let your father calm down."

I stared at him, and for a moment I wondered whom he took after. He had a thick crop of hair and dark blue eyes like mine, but he resembled none of the other children.

I knew he was mine. I gave birth to him, but what went wrong to make him so angry and disrespectful? I wiped my sweaty hands on my housedress.

"Why on Earth did you steal a car?" He started stammering which he did whenever he was thinking of a good answer. "What happened, Jim?"

"W-well, Danny Ryan and I were in front of St. Peters church on Concord Ave. There was a brand new Chevy, red and white, with the top down. W-we thought it looked pretty nice, and Danny dared me to drive it. I knew I could hot wire it and go for a ride."

"It looked s-safe enough, no one was around. They must've been at Mass. So, we jumped in, hit the gas, and took off to Harvard Square. H-honest! I was going to return it, Ma! But, just before the Square we heard sirens and that chicken shit, Danny, jumped out."

"Well the cops grabbed me and handcuffed me and roughed me up a bit," he said, rubbing his arm. "They should have let me go. Not a big deal. . . . Like I said, I was gonna return it."

"You're probably going to jail for this."

He shrugged his shoulders at me. "Your father's inside, calling Max Berger, our attorney. I don't know how it will turn out. But I do know you were never brought up to steal. I don't think your father will forgive you this time."

Max Berger defended him. Gordon ironically believed Jewish attorneys were not influenced by anything other than justice. Jim got justice all right, and six months in Billerica Penitentiary. Gordon fumed for weeks.

"I could have given him a loan for a car. He did it to embarrass me."

"I've always thought he needed help, a psychiatrist," I replied.

"Oh, bullshit, Gladys. What he needs is a swift kick in the ass. Now he'll have a police record. No one ever made it easy for me, and I never stole a dime."

I rode the bus to Billerica whenever I could to visit him. It was an hour journey each way. There was nothing out there except a few cow farms. Sue went with me several times. At night it was a dark journey. As I looked out the large window, all I saw was a tired, disappointed face staring back at me.

Jim was glad to see me but he blamed everyone but himself for stealing. Gordon never went to see him. I blamed him for being so hard on Jim but I knew there was no excuse for what Jim did. So in the end Jim was the first to leave the house, for a six-month stay at Billerica Penitentiary.

CHAPTER 44

FAREWELL TO LUCY

1944
GLADYS

It was 1944 and Gordon thought the war would be over in another year. The phone rang, a sharp urgent staccato. It was my niece Bette with sad news.

"Oh, Aunt Gladys. It's my mother, she died in hospital today."

"What? No, it can't be true." A cold shudder of dread encompassed me.

"What happened, Bette?"

Through her tears and sobs she told me the tragic story.

"Ma took Georgie to the Salvation Army picnic. You know she's an active member of the Salvation Army Church."

"On the way back, at the train station, Georgie started misbehaving and fell onto the tracks. A man reached down and dragged him up the four-foot drop from the tracks by his arm just as the train appeared."

"Thank God he's safe, your Mom must have been beside herself."

"That's just it, Aunt Glad, she wasn't herself after that. I got home from school and she was lying down. She could hardly speak. I couldn't understand her. Her words were slurred and her mouth was all crooked. I ran upstairs to the landlady while Georgie stayed with Ma. The landlady took one look at her and said, 'Stroke.' She called an ambulance to take her to Mercy Hospital."

My heart sunk at the word stroke. I felt the full impact of the seriousness of her condition, if it was indeed a stroke.

"She waved us away and said the County Hospital. Aunt Gladys, I don't know why she would go to the County Hospital when she worked at Mercy? It just doesn't make sense."

"June came to see her in hospital. Dad was there. She said Ma waved him away when he leaned over to kiss her. She bent over the bedrail to tell her she loved her and was praying for her, and she was astonished at how black and blue my mother's face was. She looked as if she'd been punched in the mouth. Her mouth was twisted, and we couldn't understand a word she said."

I covered the mouthpiece of the phone as I sobbed inwardly.

"Aunt Gladys, she's gone. She's dead." Bette sobbed uncontrollably.

My heart went out to her, and I felt my own heart crushing against my ribcage.

"Oh Bette dear, I'm so sorry, I just can't believe it. I can't imagine her gone."

"June packed all her things this morning and moved out. You know Don left home a few years ago, so it's just Irene, Georgie, and me now. My father is always angry and drinking, and I don't want to be alone with him."

"Would you come, Aunt Gladys? I think Don will take care of all the arrangements."

"Of course I will," I replied.

The next day I phoned Heber and Sue, and then I called Newfoundland. Father was heartbroken. Lucy was such a good person, she deserved better. She never got back to Twillingate. Hilda was young when Lucy left but we all remembered her as a kind-hearted sister.

A black limousine pulled up outside the church. The Salvation Army had arranged everything for the funeral. She gave so much of her time to them. The service was a small affair but a lovely tribute to Lucy. They did a nice job, and were all dressed up in their Salvation Army outfits. Flower arrangements were placed along the aisles and altar. The group sang some beautiful hymns including, *Amazing Grace, Bye and Bye*, and *Rock of Ages*. The pastor spoke of all the good Lucy had done for the poor. We held hands, sang with them, and wept.

I couldn't help but think about her hard life, working all the time, always a mouth to feed, a house to clean, and a husband that had a hard time keeping a job. When he was drinking, he was abusive. Poor Luce, she was always helping those in need, but no one helped her.

It would be up to Bette now to care for Irene, Georgie, and her father. I knew how hard that would be for her. Her two siblings had left home. June would always be supportive to Bette, but she had little to do with her father.

It was a sad day indeed. Gordon and I went home that evening and I held him close to me as I felt waves of loss for poor Lucy and her family. In the meantime I had a houseful of my own family to worry about, and Jim coming home from jail.

CHAPTER 45

TWILLINGATE REVISITED

1946
GLADYS

Twillingate called to me; it was time for another visit. I still regretted that I hadn't been able to go when my mother passed away in 1936. Now I was anxious to see my father and Twillingate once again. Gordon went with me and we made plans to visit his sister Eva and the family in Heart's Delight.

We took young Gordon, my sister Sue, and her daughter Audrey with us. My sister Hilda and her husband Captain Peter Troake lived in a historic two-story home, originally built and owned by Captain Ephraim Jacobs in 1881. Their son Jack was about the same age as Gordon, and Audrey was slightly older. Elizabeth, named after her departed grandmother, was a toddler and their daughter Doreen had not been born yet.

This time we enjoyed a smooth ferry crossing. Twillingate lay like a sparkling gem in the sunlight just ahead of us. It was summer and the weather was mild. In the far distance I could make out what seemed to be an iceberg. Crystal blue skies, sunshine, and a gentle breeze met us at the dock along with my family.

They stood in a line, waving. Home! My heart filled, and tears welled in my eyes. Gordon wrapped his arm around me. Sue cried too. It felt like a lifetime since I had been back. The smells of the sea filled my lungs and the sounds of the gulls overhead brought me home again.

We were astounded at the changes. New homes had sprouted up everywhere, and the pier was crowded with dories. A new hustle and bustle greeted us on the wharf.

We hugged and kissed and cried. What an emotional day for all of us.

"We're having a big feed at our house," piped in Hilda between all the hugs. "Fish and brewis, cherry cake, partridge berries. Just like the meals you grew up with."

"Can't wait!" Sue and I said at the same time.

Father had aged. He was a little sadder looking since the loss of my mother. But he still kept a good stride as we walked the familiar road to our childhood home. Gordon patted my father on the back.

"Good to be here."

"Good to see you again, we're not getting any younger, son." Audrey and Gordon tramped along snickering and sharing some joke. The two of them were devil skins. I hope they behaved. I'm sure Sue thought the same.

During our stay we visited with more family and old friends, while Sue went to her husband Frank's family with Audrey. We ate large down-home traditional dinners until we were stuffed to the point of bursting.

Not without a show of protest, young Gordon was pleased as punch to meet all his cousins and some local girls who thought he was a celebrity.

"From the States are you? Tell us all about it!" they would chime in.

Our visit flew by, and soon it was time to say goodbye and spend a couple of days in Heart's Delight with Gordon's family. Audrey and Sue would stay with Father until we returned two days later.

We took the train to Heart's Delight and I remembered my trip all those years ago, pregnant and dragging an uncooperative Jim with me to meet Gordon's sister. My parents had been right all along; I needed to go back to Gordon. I had made the right choice and never regretted it.

Gordon had a surprise for his sister Eva. He had ordered a wringer washer and a refrigerator to be delivered from Sears, Roebuck & Co. Eva was ecstatic. Eva had two children; they were both grown-up and married. She named her son Gordon, after her brother. He married Mary, an orphan. Mary was the most pleasant person ever created. She worked like a servant, baking bread in the old iron stove, a pair of threadbare men's briefs over her thick red hair, scuffling around pleasantly and making tea for everyone.

Eva's husband Ambrose sat in the homemade oak rocker by the cast iron stove rocking away, while Mary and Eva waited on him. But Eva was the matriarch with a capital M. She ruled the household and her children. Gordon and Mary had an opportunity to buy a small home on the same road and the owner would have financed it for them. Eva told them if they left her house she would never step foot across their threshold. So, they stayed under her roof abiding by her rules.

Eva was proud of Gordon. She beamed when she saw him. He loved her like a mother, which she pretty much was. She saved him from being sent to the orphanage and he made her proud. Mary and Gordon gave up their bed for us and they slept on the feather mattress in the attic. They insisted on it . . . or maybe it was Eva who insisted.

All too soon we would be going home. Many hugs and tears later we picked up Sue and Audrey and headed back to Boston.

CHAPTER 46

PRISCILLA JAYNE HARNUM

1947
GLADYS

Autumn has always been my favorite season, with trees bursting into yellow, red, or orange foliage. The air was crisp, not cold. I would be forty before long. Something was unsettling inside of me. I felt very broody. It couldn't be . . . but Dr. Poirier confirmed it. I was pregnant. My husband came into the kitchen and stared at me.

"What's wrong now, Gladys?" My eyes were a dead giveaway.

"Oh Gordon, we're expecting another baby."

He laughed and pulled me to him. "What's one more? We can afford it now, and finally you have time to enjoy a baby. When are you due?"

"End of May. Dr. Poirier insisted on a Caesarean because of what happened with Bill."

"Is that dangerous?"

"Oh, no. It's just such a relief, I thought you might be upset."

"Glad, you know me better than that." He hugged me close.

Uldine and Louise seemed rattled when I told them the good news. I knew they really couldn't believe their parents were still intimate at our age. I thought they were just mostly embarrassed for us.

"Mother, you're almost forty. Isn't that dangerous?" the girls chimed in.

Typical Dot. "Ma, not another brat at your age?"

The boys didn't care one way or the other.

Because it would be a Caesarean, I could choose a day at the end of May for the birth. Young Gordon's birthday was the twenty-eighth and the doctor thought that was a perfect day, but I wanted this baby to have his or her own birthday. So I chose May 22nd.

My family gathered around me in the hospital, just as I was coming out of the anesthesia.

"Congratulations!" they all chimed in. "It's a girl!"

And so, on May 22, I had a beautiful strawberry blonde, blue-eyed baby girl. We named her Priscilla Jayne, Priscilla after Gordon's Newfoundland half-sister, and Jayne after a favorite niece from Newfoundland.

She was the light of my life.

The family would kid me that Priscilla's strawberry color had something to do with Red the Baker. My father and sister both had reddish hair, so luckily that rumor didn't last long!

CHAPTER 47

THE BOYS

1940-50s
GLADYS

NEIL JAMES

Jim had come home from his incarceration at Billerica in 1945, and went to work at the shop. Bob, one of Gordon's nephews, worked there with Uncle Bill. The three of them all seemed "too closely related." They possessed a negative attitude and were prone to bad-mouth and gossip. It was a bad match. They did their job, but added no positive energy to their environment.

Soon after another disagreement with his father, Jim applied for a job at a factory in Watertown. He met an assembly line worker by the name of Anna. She was a timid Polish girl raised by her sister. She lost both parents at a young age. Dark-haired and nervous, but always pleasant, I was happy for them, and glad that Jim had moved on from working at the shop. I prayed it would all work out for them.

Gordon never brought up any of Jim's past. In fact, he was never one to remind any of the children of any past troubles. I admired him for that. Jim wanted to open a welding shop. He talked to me about it first. He wouldn't ask his father for money to start it, but he knew I would ask for him. Gordon willingly gave Jim enough to open a small garage and buy welding tools. I think Jim felt his father owed it to him, but Gordon just wanted his son to succeed and make a good living. He loved all his children.

Jim and Anna were married at St. James's Church. I felt a wave of hope that he would straighten out and create a good life for himself.

YOUNG GORDON

As unfair as it seemed, Gordon was the favorite son. He graduated from high school at sixteen like his sister Louise. They both skipped two grades. After graduation he begged his father to allow him to enlist in the Air Force. Gordon declined. He felt he was too young.

"Gordon, you should go to college. I'll pay for everything. Please just consider it." But he said no. He was determined to enlist in the Air Force. On his seventeenth birthday he was still just as determined, so Gordon capitulated and finally signed for him to enlist. After his training, he was stationed in California.

BILL

I left on a short trip and worried about leaving Gordon and the kids alone. Gordon usually left for work by 6 a.m. It was Dot's job to rouse Bill out of bed and get him off to school. Bill always needed prodding. He spent way too much time in the woods fishing and trapping, or daydreaming - something he'd far rather do than attend school.

That morning he pleaded sick with Dot. "I'm really sick. I'm not faking it."

"Get your ass out of bed. There's nothing wrong with you," she chastised.

"Honest, I'm not faking it, Dot."

Dot took a close look at him and felt his forehead. He was burning up.

"Gee, I'll go get Mrs. Mossey. Maybe you really are sick."

Mrs. Mossey was quick to diagnose the need for the doctor. Dr. Poirier was soon at the house and said Bill needed to go to the hospital.

"I think it's meningitis. Call your father. I'll talk to him."

Thank goodness for Dr. Poirier. Bill had meningitis and was lucky to be alive.

CHAPTER 48

THE GIRLS

1940s-1950
GLADYS

ULDINE

My sweet quiet daughter was getting dressed for her senior prom when Gordon popped his head in the doorway.

"Uldine, if you're not home by midnight the doors will be locked. You tell that friend of yours, Howie, I said so. He better have you home by twelve. Don't mean to spoil a good time, but if you're not home by midnight . . ."

"You hear me?"

"Yes, Dad. I understand. I'll tell Howard. He'll be here soon enough, you can tell him yourself."

"No need to, I think he knows me well enough by now." Gordon gave a little smile behind her back.

It was barely after midnight when they got home, but as promised the doors were locked. Howard had to feel his way around the backyard in the pitch dark until he found the old wooden ladder and leaned it up against the porch. He and Uldine pushed it up to the girls' bedroom window. As she crawled up to the window, her lovely blue prom dress dragged in the dew and caught on the rough edges of the ladder, ruining the hem of the skirt. *Tap-tap.* Louise and Dot were waiting to let her in.

Uldine and Howie married in 1950, the first of my daughters' weddings. She looked lovely and happy as her father walked her down the aisle at St. James's. Her two sisters and Audrey were bridesmaids and her baby sister Priscilla was the flower girl - she was only three years old.

By May of 1951 Uldine was expecting her first child. She delivered a tiny girl. Kathy was premature and needed an incubator. Cambridge City Hospital didn't have one. The doctor asked Howard if he would take the baby to Boston City Hospital where they had incubators.

Howie with only one good arm couldn't carry the baby and drive all the way to the hospital alone. He picked-up his sister Betty and they got tiny baby Kathy from the hospital and drove her to Boston City where they kept her in an incubator until she could go home.

LOUISE

Louise was the beautiful confident daughter, and Gordon's favorite. She would graduate at sixteen. So smart, she skipped two grades. She was always poised and confident. She was also a Daddy's girl and she often rode along with her father while he estimated a job. She was still dating Fred who was madly in love with her, but she was in no hurry to become a wife and mother. However, after four years of Fred's persistence he finally won her over. (Along with the help of a new belt!) He had enlisted in the Air Force and they spent their honeymoon in Texas where he was based.

DOROTHY

It was late in the afternoon and Dot snuck into the house, dripping wet from swimming at Jerry's Pit - something they were never allowed to do. She climbed the stairs to the girls' bedroom for a change of dry clothes.

"Why are you all wet, what are you up to now?" Louise quizzed her.

"I almost drowned!"

"What do you mean?"

"Me and the kids from Sherman Street swam under the chain-link fence to swim at the Pit."

"You know you're not supposed to go there."

"I know, but we did. The other kids swam under the chain-link fence before me but I got caught. Thought I was gonna drown, Louise. I pulled out my falsies, the ones you always make fun of, and they floated right to the surface. The kids saw them floating away and came under the fence and pulled me free. I almost died!"

"Good thing you're so flat-chested, you have to wear falsies. Honestly Dot, why do you do such crazy things? I'm glad you're okay though. NEVER go there again and I won't tell Mother."

About this time Dot had a boyfriend named John. A very nice man, but he seemed more like a girlfriend than a boyfriend. Louise, normally a kind person, just had to poke fun at Dot about John.

"He's a bit funny, you know."

"No, he's not!" Dot came at her, ready to punch it out.

"Has he ever even attempted first base?"

"None of your BI business. You're just getting even because I made fun of Fred and his stupid belt."

"Not so. Just think about it."

John was indeed "a bit funny," but Dot and John remained friends for years, even after she married Tom.

Photos on page 118
Eldest children with Gordon and Gladys at Revere Beach circa 1935
On steps of Locke Street early 1940s
High School photos (top) Uldine, Louise, Gordon; (bottom) Dot, Bill, Priscilla
Portrait (clockwise from top left) Bill, Jim, Uldine, Gordon, Priscilla, Dot, Louise

1950s

CHAPTER 49

TRAIN TO AMARILLO

WINTER 1953
GLADYS

In 1951 Fred, my son-in-law, had enlisted in the Air Force. After they married in 1952, he and Louise settled down to a military life in off-base housing near Amarillo, Texas. My daughter's letters arrived weekly, filled with details of their interesting life in Texas. But I could read between the lines and knew how much she missed her family and home.

It was another cold, gloomy, winter day out. I sat looking out the window and wondering when the snow would stop. The phone interrupted my thoughts. It was Louise.

"Why don't you get out of the snow and come for a visit, Mom? Fred is at the base all day and we have friends, but it's not like having your family. You could take the train. I know how much you hate to fly. . . . Oh, please?"

"I don't know, Louise, it's such a long way from here, and I have Priscilla to take care of. Your father is busy right now with the business, and he can't watch her. I'm not saying no, but let me think about it."

At dinner I mentioned it to Gordon.

"Well, what do you think, Gordon?"

"Go! Louise misses you, and you're due for a holiday. Think of it as an adventure. Maybe Sue will go with you and help with Priscilla. Why don't you ask her?"

Sue was delighted with the idea of going. She hadn't been anywhere since she came to the States. Good with travel details, Louise made all the reservations.

The snow on the ground was melting, but there was still a

cold frost in the air and an icy crunch on the ground. I would be glad to get out of the cold for a while.

We were headed to Texas, where the sun was shining and the snow rarely, if ever, fell or so we thought. Priscilla carried her red patent-leather suitcase packed with her Ginny dolls and all their outfits. We traveled light, just a coat and a small travel bag each. I had a small suitcase with Priscilla's clothes.

The train would be traveling on part of the route of the Atchison, Topeka and Santa Fe Railroad. We were in high spirits and on the way to the station, we sang the famous song by Johnny Mercer, *"On the Atchison, Topeka and the Santa Fe."* Gordon dropped us off at South Station and hugged us both.

"Have a safe trip. Give Louise my love, and don't worry about anything. I'll be back to pick you up in two weeks."

"I won't worry." I smiled back at him. But of course, I would.

The trip was indeed an adventure. We made ourselves comfortable on the grey cushioned seats. It was a two-day journey, over 2,000 miles. We didn't book a berth, but we enjoyed watching cattle, cotton fields, tumbleweed, and cactus through the carriage windows.

Soldiers filled the train, all wearing different uniforms and all of varying ages. Priscilla visited them all, chatting as she walked up and down the aisles. We watched closely where she went. I had learned my lesson from the incident with Gordon and the photographer those many years ago.

She was such a gregarious, engaging child. I smiled as I watched her. Her platinum blonde hair cut in a Dutch clip stood up in places from the static. Sue bought Priscilla a Black Beauty book to read her to sleep. Priscilla loved Black Beauty and Sue sang her favorite childhood song, "I love my dog and my dog loves me. I found him under the old grey tree."

This time we changed the word dog to horse.

Louise and Fred were at the station with open arms, and there were tears in Louise's eyes, she was that happy to see us. I was very happy to see her too. Fred looked thin. Handsome in his Air Force blues, his pale blue eyes reflecting the color of his uniform. Louise had gone on the fad RX Diet and had lost all her chubbiness. Not that I ever thought she needed to lose weight. She looked svelte and somehow more sophisticated.

We arrived dusty and tired to their off-base housing, a small two-bedroom apartment located just outside of Amarillo. Sue and I shared the spare bedroom. Louise liked to bake and Fred liked to cook and so we were introduced to Texan and Mexican cuisine. The meals were spicy but quite good.

Our first adventure was a trip to Juarez, Mexico. The streets were filled with locals, loose roosters, and stray dogs. Native vendors hawked large straw sombreros and noisy maracas. Alongside on makeshift tables lay brightly painted bowls of pottery. I watched, fascinated while the local women chatted away at a fast clip in Spanish. The pungent smell of overripe food and sweat pervaded the market. Wooden bushel baskets were filled with beans, limes, and a variety of hot peppers. Sacks of cornmeal and rice were stacked up next to them, the staples of Mexico.

The locals kept patting Priscilla on her blonde head. She didn't seem to mind, and Louise said it was for good luck because she was so fair. At lunch in the cantina a mariachi band serenaded us. Dancers holding castanets or maracas twirled their flouncy skirts. Vibrant colors of yellow, red, green, and gold swirled around us as they moved with the music. A group of the locals brought out roosters and cocks tied to their wrists, and did a mock cock fight.

That was a bit too much for me. Shaking our heads, we declined when they thought we might like to see a real bull fight. After lunch, we piled into the car and took off. On the way home, out of nowhere we were hit by a blizzard. Snowdrifts were piling up everywhere. I shuddered as we drove by cows frozen in the fields. Fred drove slowly, but I was such a nervous person I prayed for our safe return. The blizzard left a record snowfall.

Just like that, the next day the snow was almost melted. Louise dropped Fred off at the base and we headed to a store to buy boots. We got the last pair of children's boots, a bright pair of red cowboy boots for Priscilla. She loved them.

As we walked home, we saw a man wearing a cowboy hat and boots. He stepped out of the dry cleaners, located only a few feet from our apartment, his arms were full of clean shirts. There was a hitching post outside the cleaners, and as he went by, he winked and tipped his hat at Priscilla. She was an inquisitive child and I told her that a hitching post was used for parking your horse. I told her that it probably had real horses tied up to it at one time. After that, Priscilla would go out there each day with her jump rope and pretend to tie up her imaginary horse. I laughed because she talked as if there actually was a horse there. From that day on, all Priscilla wanted was a horse.

CHAPTER 50

ENTER EARL

MAY 1953
GLADYS

In the spring of 1953 my daughter Uldine went into labor. Her husband Howard drove her to Somerville Hospital. They were expecting an uneventful delivery. The placenta came out first and then a baby boy. He had stopped breathing and the staff presumed he was dead. It was not an uncommon occurrence back in the 1950s. The staff immediately turned their attention to Uldine.

She started hemorrhaging, and her blood pressure had dropped so low it was life threatening. Uldine had two children at home that needed her alive, Kathy and Wendy. The doctors went to work on her immediately. At some point during the emergency, the "assumed dead" baby coughed. He was alive! But by then the poor boy had suffered a severe loss of oxygen. Due to the damage, he would never be able to walk, or talk more than a few words.

It was almost more than Howard was willing to accept. It might be considered malpractice now, but no one sued back in those days. Many preventable tragedies were just considered an act of God. You just dealt with it, and so they did. They named him Earl and they loved him just like they loved all their other children.

CHAPTER 51

FAREWELL TO FATHER

1953
GLADYS

My sister Hilda was on the phone to us one evening. Father had taken a turn for the worse and was dying. Priscilla was only six and I hated to leave her, but it only made sense to leave her with Mrs. Mossey across Chetwynd Road. Gordon could watch over Dot and Bill.

Heber and I caught a flight to Gander but we were too late. Father passed away before we arrived. He was in his mid-eighties. The entire island came to mourn and honor him. We buried him beside our dear mother.

CHAPTER 52

THE CAPE - MARION

1954
GLADYS

When the children were young, Gordon had rented a cottage at Swift's Beach in Wareham, Massachusetts. It was considered "Upper Cape Cod." We had friends from Newfoundland who settled in Wareham, both the Skinners and the Egglestons.

It was a wonderful time for the children as well as adults to escape the summer heat of the city, and spend time on the beach. The kids ran around the yard playing tag and running under the hose. During our vacations, Dot tripped over a bucket in the garden and managed to break her arm, twice, two summers in a row! Other than that it was uneventful. I never did learn to swim, so I would sit on the beach with my eyes peeled on the blonde heads of my children, warning them not to go any further than their knees.

One Sunday morning in 1954 at the house in Cambridge, Gordon was drinking his coffee and perusing the classified section of the Boston Globe. He read out loud.

"Dexter Beach, building lots for sale $500.00 each, located in Marion."

"I think we should go look at these lots, Glad. Sounds like a great price to me. My friend Vin is a builder. He lives in the next town over. He could build a cottage on one of the lots for us. Let's drive down there next weekend. It sounds perfect! Don't ya think, Glad?"

"It would be nice, Gordon, if we can afford it."

"I'll call Vin and Bessie Skinner right now and tell them we're coming. We will take a look around Marion and then stop by Vin's for a visit."

The next Saturday we took the Pontiac Bonneville and drove down with Dot and Priscilla.

It was an hour and half drive. Not bad. Walter Dexter was the gentleman who owned the lots. We called and arranged to meet him to view the property.

CHAPTER 53

MARION, MASSACHUSETTS

Marion was once known as Sippican, after the Wampanoag tribe. Their leader was the great Indian chief Massasoit in Buzzards Bay and they enjoyed the abundance of oysters the bay provided. Around 1678 twenty-nine Pilgrim families settled in the area. Thanks to warm relations between Massasoit and the Pilgrim leaders, the Indians and the white settlers remained friendly for many years.

Independence
After the Pilgrims arrival in 1620 land grants were issued to Marion, Mattapoisett and parts of Wareham. The name Rochester was chosen because many of the original settlers had come from Rochester, England. In 1852, after several years of bickering between the villages, Marion became a separate town. Instead of keeping the Indian name, Sippican, the settlers chose the name Marion in honor of General Francis Marion, a Revolutionary War hero from South Carolina.

Seafaring Industry
By the early 1800s Marion was a small but thriving seacoast town. Marion's chief products were professional sailors who sailed on whaling ships, coastal schooners, and Liverpool packets. Marion tended more toward whaling and producing sea captains than making money from shipbuilding. Some became very wealthy and built magnificent homes in Marion. Captain Benjamin Briggs, of the brig Mary Celeste, stands out in maritime history in what may be the greatest unsolved mystery

of the sea, the disappearance of the entire crew of the Mary Celeste between the Azores and Portugal in 1872.

Legacy of a Lady

As the whaling industry went into decline thanks to the discovery of oil, Marion was being run by a group of stubborn old sea captains who did not believe in education and change. It took the will and generosity of a formidable lady - Elizabeth Pitcher Taber - to revive the declining town of Marion. Following her husband's death, Elizabeth, now a wealthy widow, returned to her hometown with a mission to revive the town. She established the Elizabeth Taber library and the Natural History Museum; she built what is now known as the Music Hall; and she contributed a significant sum to build the Marion Town Hall. She also established the Tabor Academy, named after Mount Tabor near the Sea of Galilee.

The Rise of Tourism

The railroad also brought changes to Marion. The trains to Marion began bringing people from Boston and New York who wanted to spend a vacation on the unspoiled sandy white seashore, away from the heat of the city summer. Wealthy families like the Stone Family built mansions. Others from as far away as Chicago arrived with steamer trunks, valises, hatboxes, and carry-alls. They bought big, beautiful summer homes, many of which are still standing and lived in by the same wealthy families. By the 1880s Marion became a nationally known resort for the rich and famous and it remained such for many years.

Excerpts courtesy of Sippican Historical Society, used with permission.

CHAPTER 54

DEXTER BEACH

1954
GLADYS

Back in the 1950s Dexter Beach was a tract of land consisting of about 400 acres. It sold in small cottage lots for $500.00 per lot. The land, located on the far side of the town of Marion, was set against the Weweantic River that flowed into Buzzards Bay. The area was commonly referred to as Upper Cape Cod.

The price of lots and the charm of the town not only attracted Gordon, but attracted many middle class workers, businessmen, and families from locales all around Boston. However, the beach in this area was not a real beach at all, just tall sawgrass and marsh leading out to the Weweantic and Buzzards Bay.

We pulled up to the address that Walter Dexter, the owner, gave us. We had a good walk around the entire property; Gordon seemed keener than ever to purchase the lots. I was less eager when I realized they had no beach access. Walter, a kind weathered man, widowed, and living in a single-family, cedar-shingle cape, at the entrance gave us a brief but proud history of the town of Marion and his family.

Despite my misgivings, Gordon saw opportunity and the means to make the marshy sawgrass into a real beach. He had the heavy equipment and the know-how to create a pristine white beach within walking distance of the lots. After listening to Walter Dexter's stories about Marion, Gordon was just as eager to buy as Mr. Dexter was to sell, and the deal was made.

CHAPTER 55

HURRICANE CAROL

August 31, 1954
GLADYS

We were in the process of building the new cottage in Marion, but it would be months before it would be completed. Gordon rented a small bungalow for us in Wareham, the next town over from Marion. The tiny two-bedroom rental fronted on a grassy patch of beach with a magnificent view of Buzzards Bay.

That summer I invited Florence Schoffield to come down and stay with Priscilla and me. "Florrie" was an English lady from our church back home. I wouldn't have stayed alone anyway, so it worked out well enough. Gordon came down on the weekends when he could to work on the new cottage.

To while the time away during the week while Gordon worked in Boston, Florrie and I played Canasta. It was a Monday after a whirlwind visit from Gordon. We sat inside at the card table, and looked out over the sawgrass and the bay. As we played cards, I saw the sky begin to darken and the wind pick up.

"Look! I think we're in for a bad storm, Florrie."

I was afraid of lightning since a childhood friend had been struck and killed while reading the Sears catalog in an outhouse. I didn't want Priscilla to be afraid too.

Lightning flashed as I spoke, a clap of thunder boomed, and we all jumped. Poor Priscilla, she hung on to my skirt, her eyes as big as saucers. She had goose bumps and the electric static caused her hair to stand up on her head.

"We're going to need to unplug anything electrical. Priscilla, help me. Let's carry the card table inside."

Florrie sat on shuffling the deck of cards.

"Oh bother! It's just a bit of a storm, Gladys."

As I sat there watching the pounding rain, Florrie sat in the kitchen, methodically dealing her precious Canasta cards. Fearless old lady, I thought to myself.

It started to rain harder, and the wind blew the lawn chairs across the street. I spotted our neighbors waving furiously in our direction.

"Florrie, the people across the road are waving for us to come there. Let's get out of here. The storm is getting stronger. Look, the waves are washing right up to the cottage now."

The wind was so violent it sounded as if it would rip the roof off. I ran around and grabbed my purse and then the silliest items, my electric iron, a hairbrush, a reluctant Florrie, and of course Priscilla. Priscilla and I had to hold hands with the frail Florrie. As we crossed over the road, the wind nearly lifted her off the ground.

The neighbors looked a bit disappointed when they realized we were not the owners who they were friendly with, but just rental strangers. As we crossed the street we saw a huge white house bobbing like a cork, floating across Buzzards Bay. Reluctantly they invited us in and told us this was a "real hurricane."

But as the storm increased its intensity we knew we had to head for higher ground. We left, moving to higher ground as the water washed over the doorstep in waves.

We rushed up the flooded road and then headed up the hill. A truck pulled up beside us. It was the evacuation truck. They told us to get in the truck bed. We obeyed instantly, clambering in the back as the wind nearly blew us away.

The truck carried us along with the other cold and wet survivors to the Wareham Town Hall. Hundreds of people were taking refuge there. Hot coffee, ham sandwiches, and blueberry muffins were handed out to all. Priscilla, my fussiest eater, didn't like ham sandwiches or blueberry muffins so she went hungry.

The volunteers arranged for us to get a lift back to Cambridge by bus. We looked like wet refugees with my electric iron hanging out of my purse. As we left Wareham behind, it looked like a disaster zone. Downed power lines spewed sparks into the street. Trees and branches blocked the roads.

We arrived home safe to Cambridge that afternoon, only to find that Gordon had gone.

GORDON

Gordon stepped down hard on the gas pedal and the back wheels burned rubber. Normally a safe driver, he was in a hurry to get to the Cape cottage and rescue his family. His heart pounded harder with every mile he drove. After a few wrong turns and a few blocked streets he got through to the rental cottage.

"Gladys!! GLADYS!!"

He yelled for Gladys at the top of his lungs as he jumped out of the truck. No answer. He walked up stunned as he surveyed the damage. The wind had died down and the water had settled back towards the bay. There was no sign of his family or any survivors. Surely, they had all been washed out to sea. It wasn't possible they survived the massive damage of the hurricane.

The first thing he noticed was the total devastation left by the hurricane. Houses that had no roofs and rooms that had no walls. It was like looking into a cutout house.

In a state of shock he noted the wreckage. Homes were in a shambles, some lifted by the surge onto their neighbor's property or across the marshes. Beds were turned upside-down; there were chests without drawers, tables without chairs. Their rental cottage had no foundation, but that was its salvation. It had completely filled with ocean water, and then as the storm subsided the water drained off, leaving the interior furnishings strewn about. In a daze Gordon looked upward only to see Florrie's Canasta cards had floated and stuck to the ceiling!

Weeping, he drove until he could find a phone booth. He called Dot to tell her the terrible news. The phone rang and Dot picked it up, but before she could say anything Gordon sobbed into the phone.

"They're gone, they're all gone!"

"No, Dad," she shouted over his sobs. "No, Dad, they're all here and they're safe."

Hurricane Carol caused widespread destruction of buildings, automobiles, boats, and crops. Power was out for days and martial law declared. Over 150,000 people were left without electricity and phone service. The name "Carol" was retired for a decade after it struck in 1954.

CHAPTER 56

BILL JOINS UP

1954
GLADYS

My son Bill was in his last year of high school and we knew he was thinking of his next move. We expected him to choose a college, and one hopefully nearby.

What we didn't expect was the little bomb he dropped at the dinner table one evening.

"Dad, when I graduate I'm going to enlist in the Army."

"I thought you wanted to work in the business?" quizzed Gordon.

"I will Dad when I get out of the Army in four years."

"I thought at least one of my kids would go to college," Gordon muttered under his breath, but loud enough for Bill to hear him.

"None of my friends are going to college, Dad. I'll get to see the world this way."

"Hmm . . . no guarantee of that, son. Best to finish high school, you may change your mind. You won't be trapping and fishing in the Army, I can tell you that."

At this point I could tell that Gordon thought the same thing as me. Bill loved to trap. I could see his flat boards laid out with the skins of muskrat and mink hanging in our basement to dry. Bill enjoyed trekking through the woods, catching brook trout, and trapping for hides. Bill would be eighteen soon and we wouldn't have a say in it anyway. Bill was more of a loner than his brothers, but always easy to please. He was the youngest of the boys.

After dinner Gordon looked at me and shook his head.

"Where did the years go, Glad? All grown-up and leaving us. Well, we still have Dot and Priscilla."

Around that time Dot was still living with us and she worked at a bank on State Street in Boston. She was still dating John. Personally, I didn't see that going anywhere. John was pretty entertaining though. . . . I gave him that. He would try on all of our hats and prance around the living room impersonating us and making us fall over with laughter. Gordon ignored the show if he was around.

CHAPTER 57

NEW ADDITIONS

1954 -1955
GLADYS

Not long after Hurricane Carol we got a phone call from Louise and Fred. I was glad to be out of harm's way after the hurricane, and looking forward to Louise's return from Amarillo.

"Mother, we have wonderful news. Fred and I are coming home for good and we're bringing you a little package. We're expecting a baby in January, maybe on my birthday, or maybe even on your birthday, Mom. Isn't it great? You're going to be a grandmother again. We'll be back by late spring with the baby."

I was ecstatic. It gave me a great sense of relief to know they were moving back.

"That's wonderful news, Louise. I'm looking forward to it. You know I miss you terribly, Fred too of course. I just can't believe how lucky I am you're back home, plus a baby. I bet Fred is glad to be getting out of the service."

"Oh, you know Fred, Mom, he actually enjoyed his tour of duty in the Air Force."

"I know he is a good husband, and he loves you very much," I said.

"He does and I'm blessed, but to be honest I'm glad to be leaving Texas. I miss the seasons and most of all I miss the family."

"Uldine and Howie are planning a trip to Texas," I told her. "You know that?"

"Yes, I'm excited for her. She needs a change of scenery. Long trip though, but I'm glad she's coming, plus she'll be first to see the new baby."

We chatted away for a while and then we rang off. I sat back thinking about all my children. They meant everything to me. I've always had a strong sense of family and enjoyed the dynamics of our large family life. I felt truly content.

By this time my oldest daughter Uldine had four children, including the new baby Brian. I was concerned about her; she had one baby after the next. She looked thin and worn out. Although Howie was a good provider, he could be very demanding. He expected her to iron his white shirts every day to wear to work. I wished she'd get a driver's license at least, that way she could get out and go for a drive, take a break.

I would go over sometimes and help her wash the mountains of diapers, but I knew she resented it. She's too proud. I bet Howie thinks I'm meddling. Well, maybe I am. I just hate seeing my children in any distress. Whenever we visit Uldine, Priscilla hates to eat there, always the fussy one. I will say though that Uldine can throw a can of Campbell's tomato soup and pasta together and call it "spaghetti!" Sometimes she cooks ground hamburger meat and calls it "American Chop Suey."

Her shelves are stocked with powdered milk, Tang, and Spam. I'll eat anything, so I grin and bear it, but I tell Priscilla to "shush." God bless her, Uldine does the best she can with the money Howie gives her.

Uldine's son Earl has been handicapped since birth. He wears a brace on his legs at night and Howie's determined to make him walk. He set up bars in the kitchen a couple of feet off the floor and encouraged him to walk over them. It's a sin to watch, but I know in his heart he's trying to help Earl.

I gave him a lot of credit for that.

CHAPTER 58

THE COTTAGE

1955
GLADYS

It was July and the summer heat had finally arrived. We loaded the Pontiac with everything we would need for the Cape. Gordon had installed a walk-up attic in the cottage so we had plenty of room for all my children and their families to stay. They each had at least one week per summer with us. Gordon worked all week and drove down Friday nights, leaving early Monday morning - a typical commute for vacation home families.

In the back seat with Priscilla sat her cocker spaniel Honey and her black and white Angora cat Fluffy. Her entourage also included Sweety and Tweety, two green and blue parakeets in a cage. Two five and dime store turtles floated in a round dish with a little green plastic palm tree on their island.

We were driving along without incident when all of a sudden Gordon slammed on the brakes. Fluffy was sitting on the back of his seat, and she dug her claws in him and he yelled out loud - "JESUS H. CHRIST!" I was shocked.

Priscilla and I started giggling uncontrollably.

By this time in our lives we had enough time and money to give Priscilla pretty much everything she wanted. I'm sure some of her siblings resented that occasionally. They had so often had to do without in the early years of our marriage.

Being a great deal younger than her brothers and sisters, Priscilla had all the dolls and toys and pets she wanted. She never did get a pony, but we bought her a Raleigh 3-speed bicycle for her birthday.

Summer at the Cape! What an exciting time for all of us. Our grandchildren were increasing in number. We had mostly grandsons but a few granddaughters too.

They would each visit for one week, and then the next group would come.

"Look, Dad," shouted Priscilla, "Harnum Way, we're here!"

Dexter Beach had one road in and one road out, Dexter Road. There were seven dirt roads that intersected it, and each road was named after the first families to buy and build. We named ours Harnum Way.

The Dorans had a road, and the Coles, and so on, and so forth.

A horn honked. It was the Scanlons.

"Hiya Gladys, we're down for the summer," they chimed in unison.

The Scanlons, Mary and Jack, had a double lot next to ours. They were from Yonkers, New York. Jack was a policeman and Mary was a nurse. They pulled a bright Pepto-Bismol pink trailer, 28 x 8 feet around. I imagine Mary picked it out, and I often wondered if Jack was embarrassed by the color.

"That's great. Priscilla is looking forward to playing with Anita."

They had a daughter Anita, a little older than Priscilla. The two of them spent rainy days inside designing paper doll clothing.

Anita jumped out of the car as it pulled up.

"Hi Cilla! I'm here for the whole summer!"

"Mom, can Anita and I go to the beach?"

"Yes, if it's alright with her mother."

Although I never got over my life-long fear of the ocean, I was at peace with it. Gordon built the beach for our family and we all enjoyed it. At high tide barefoot and tanned, Anita and Priscilla, blonde hair streaming, ran at top speed down the hill to the beach. I didn't worry. She had learned to swim and there was always an adult watching over the kids.

Every week the kids biked to the Stone Estate at Great Hill, three miles down the shoreline. They each brought lunch in a brown paper bag. Great Hill sat on a peninsula that jutted out into Buzzards Bay. It was over 100 feet above sea level and the highest point in Marion. It had a couple of miles of waterfront and 300 acres of rolling woods, meadows, and lawns.

Priscilla and her friends pulled up to the house on their bikes.

"Mom, we're going to bike down to Stone Estate."

"Okay, sounds good but be careful. Here you go." I passed out homemade brownies all around to put in their brown bag lunch.

"Thanks, Ma." "Thanks, Mrs. Harnum!" And off they went.

The kids had a routine; first they visited the barn where the cows were being milked. Immense black bulls filled the stable, with rings in their noses and names carved over their metal stalls. Blue ribbons claimed their famous lineage and breeding.

A swing hung from the ceiling about 40 feet up in the main barn. Three or four kids would be eating their bag lunch on the hay bales. Afterwards they would get on the swing, and swing high and wide through the barn.

The farm workers of Stone Estate would be busy milking the cows or feeding the workhorses or checking the chicken house for eggs. They were kind to my daughter and her friends and I made sure the kids knew to be respectful of the privilege.

The Stone family still owned the estate. Born in 1862 in Leominster, Galen Stone was the original owner. He built his castle at the high point of his property overlooking the bay. The estate had hundreds of acres, and nowadays visitors were allowed to wander through the barns and buy eggs from the egg man or walk out to the gardens. Inside the estate were rows of exotic greenhouses and beds of flowers; small goldfish ponds were filled with water lilies and frogs.

The kids rode their bikes along the shoreline and stopped at the beach house to use the changing rooms. They climbed down the rocks to the water to fetch shells and stop by the frog ponds along the way to the castle. They loved watching the dragonflies and jumping frogs.

The egg-man, the gardener, and the barn manager all had a Tudor-style home to live in provided by the Stone Family. The Stone relatives also had similar but larger Tudor homes facing the ocean. You could only view the castle from a distance, but as you approached you could see the gardens and greenhouses. One of the greenhouses had exotic plants hovering overhead and cement floors green with algae from the damp. They crossed different fruits to create uncommon varieties, and then sold them, not that they needed the money.

The Dexter Beach Association was more like a social group back then. We had barbecues and potluck dinners on the beach. We played Bingo and Canasta at night. Our group enjoyed a lot of activities, a lot of cocktails, and joking, all in good fun of course. Marion was a magical place for our children and grandchildren to grow up. Everyone knew everyone.

It was a small, intimate neighborhood. Dusk was settling in and I could hear the clink of the horseshoes as they hit the stakes at the Cohenno's house, two roads away. Laughter and shouts drifted through the air along with the fireflies.

I heard Gordon and Frank Cohenno out back and wondered what they were up to.

"Frank, throw the shells over here in this empty can."

"Sure Gordon, I can't believe it. We had an excellent catch tonight!"

Gordon and Frank were chatting away. They had been out on the bay and had harvested scallops by the bushel basket. They were shucking them out by our back door and their hands were raw. The tiny sweet scallops lived in beds only a short distance from the beach by rowboat. I couldn't wait to eat some. They were a delicious summer treat.

The kids really enjoyed summers at the Cape. Mr. Dexter the original owner was kind and generous to all of us. He had a room with a pool table, and the kids walked to his house in the evenings to play pool. They all learned how to play pretty well. They were always welcome as long as they kept it neat, shut off the lights, and closed the door behind them.

It was the end of the summer and time to head home. We had just finished packing the car. "I think that's it, Glad." Gordon securely adjusted Fluffy the cat in the back seat so we wouldn't have a repeat attack on the drive back.

As Gordon pulled away Priscilla sat in the back seat somber and looking out the rear window. With summer over, I couldn't wait for Louise and Fred to return from Texas.

CHAPTER 59

SHERMAN STREET

1955-1956
LOUISE

Fred and I were back from Amarillo and looking for a place to live in Boston. I called my mother daily, but we still hadn't been able to find an affordable place.

Finally I had some good news. I called my mother right away.

"Hi, Louise!"

"Hi, Mom! Great news, we found an apartment on Sherman Street, only a ten minute walk from Chetwynd Road."

"That's wonderful and you will be so close."

"The apartment is over a gas station, Mom."

"Oh no. It will stink, and what about all the noise? A garage!"

I knew she'd be disappointed.

"Stop worrying, Mom, it's what we can afford. It's close to you and Dad and we can walk to everything. Fred can tinker with his old car with the mechanics down on the lot. Really Mom, it's perfect for now."

"Fred starts at the shop next week, and it's fine for a while. We're grateful to you and Dad, but I want him to do something else. Family business never works out for the in-laws."

"But you know we love Fred, he's so helpful and handy. Plus he can fix just about anything. Maybe your Father can climb a skyscraper dear, but he can't fix a toilet," Ma joked.

She backed off and changed the subject, "How's little David?"

As we spoke my son David crawled around my feet. He had

all the pots and pans out of the cupboard and was banging away, always a busy little boy.

"He's good, Ma. He's a sturdy child, strong for his age, and handsome. I'm blessed he's healthy, but gracious, Ma, he's into everything!" Peals of delight went through the receiver as we chatted. I could imagine Mom smiling, an expert after raising seven children.

Fred worked at Dad's shop that first year. He and a crew loaded tires from freight train cars onto a flatbed truck, rolling four tires at a time. Then they were trucked to a warehouse. I was proud of our family business. No job was too small or too large for G. H. Harnum Inc. Dad had built a reputation for skilled workmanship and honesty.

Fred came home so tired at the end of a workday that many nights he fell asleep, exhausted on the floor without dinner. I wanted better than that for our family. I began browsing the Sunday classifieds in the Boston Globe.

"IBM hiring, will train. Fred you need to apply for a job at IBM."

"IBM? Forget it, they'll never hire me, Louise."

"Yes, they will, and not only that, they provide training. You know how you love to tinker, why not tinker with computers?"

"I dunno."

"Fred, apply, what do you have to lose?"

Fred was more cautious than me, but I prodded him and he listened. He went down to the IBM office in Cambridge that week and filled out an application. We didn't have a phone yet so he gave them my parents' name and number, Trobridge 6-1090.

The following Monday he came home in a great mood.

"Louise! I got hired," he shouted out as he came through the apartment door.

"I knew you would, Fred. Let's celebrate!"

I made his favorite Blondies for dessert, they were butterscotch brownies. I ran across the street to get some ice cream to top them off.

"So, the boss man told me that when he called your mother for a reference she said, 'Fred's a good honest, hardworking young man with a family to support. You should hire him, you won't go wrong.' He said she was so convincing that he hired me on her recommendation."

Fred made thirty dollars a week to start. After the first year he got a raise to sixty dollars a week because we had a growing family. We had another son Steven by then, the spitting image of Fred. Our tiny apartment was crowded. It was time for a move.

CHAPTER 60

YOUNG GORDON

1955-1956
GLADYS

Soon after Louise and Fred got settled into their new home I received a phone call from young Gordon. Just as he promised, Gordon had enlisted in the Air Force. I missed his smiling face and sense of humor. I had expected a call from him and looked forward to catching up with him.

"Gordon, how are you?"

"Mum, I'm sorry I haven't called much. The Air Force keeps me pretty busy. I'm singing in the church choir on base, did you know that?"

"Yes, that's great, you said that in your last letter."

Young Gordon had a nice singing voice, just like his father. I cut to the chase.

"What's this about a serious girlfriend? You're not thinking of staying in California, are you? Your father expects you to help run the business when you get out."

"No, I'm not staying in California. But I've got great news, Ma. I'm getting married!"

"What, are you serious? We haven't even met her yet, we don't even know who she is. You're way too young to get married, Gordon."

"No honest, Ma, it's fine. You'll like her, she's beautiful. We are not planning a big wedding. We're getting married at the Air Force Chapel. Just her mother and sister."

"Okay. Hold on a second; let me get your father. I'm sure it will be fine, it's just such a shock, that's all."

I called Gordon over to the phone and put my hand over the mouthpiece.

"It's Gordon on the phone and he has some news for you. He's getting married. I just can't believe it."

"Hiya, Dad. Did Ma tell you the news? I'm getting married. I know you're probably surprised, upset maybe. It's fine, and don't worry, I'm old enough to make the right decision."

"Damn, son, you're not even twenty-one years old yet! I'm relying on you to help with the business. You are coming back, right? You're not staying in California!" It was less a question than an order.

"No, Dad, as soon as I'm out of the service we'll be coming home."

"What's her name?"

"Pearl, Essie Pearl. I should have said that right away, but I was afraid of your reaction. She's a great lady. Beautiful, glamorous, and we're in love."

"As long as you're happy and coming home, I guess I'm happy for you. See you next spring, right? It will be good to have you back home, son."

Gordon and Pearl returned as promised in the spring. Pearl was just as beautiful as he described her. Taller than Gordon, she looked like an actress that stepped out of a Hollywood movie. Her make-up looked perfect, but for the life of us we could never figure out her brassiere.

We finally found out she wore something called a bullet bra, her bosoms ended in sharp narrow points like a rocket underneath her cashmere sweater. My daughters and I always felt a bit frumpy beside her.

Of course all the men in the family were ecstatic to meet the "Glamorous Pearl." Although we were in awe of her wardrobe, she always acted like a lady and was warm and friendly towards the family.

Gordon and Pearl rented an apartment in Belmont. She furnished it in a modern blonde mahogany suite. Stylish and blonde just like Pearl. We were invited to dinner and Pearl served us her specialty dish, mashed potatoes and gravy with well-done pork chops.

Gordon went back to work at the shop. Good looking and charismatic, he made a great salesman and asset to the company. It eased the burden on his father and gave us the opportunity to travel.

CHAPTER 61

FAREWELL TO FRANK

1957
GLADYS

"It's your sister Sue on the phone. Frank is lying in the foyer; she thinks he's dead. The ambulance is on the way." Gordon handed me the phone.

"Oh dear God, Sue, are you alright? We'll come right over."

"I think the ambulance is here," Sue said through her tears.

"We'll be there in a few minutes. Just sit tight, we will drive you to the hospital." I tried to comfort her on the phone; I grabbed my jacket and purse.

Sue was teary-eyed when we arrived, but she remained calm.

"It's his heart, I know it. He complained of a strong pain in his heart last night. We thought it was a gas pain. The ambulance men said they would try to save him." She burst into tears.

My heart skipped a few beats and I held her hand. Gordon was silent and driving faster than I would like. We reached Mass General and entered through the emergency doors just as the ambulance pulled away.

An older doctor with sad eyes came to tell Sue that Frank had died of a massive heart attack. He gave her his condolences. I could see she was in shock. She just stood there, eyes wide, not knowing what to say or do.

"Would you like to see him, to say goodbye?" he asked.

"Yes, please."

We accompanied her down the hall, past the emergency entrance. He wasn't covered with a sheet and I was a little shocked because I thought he would be. He looked sound asleep. His lips were blue, but otherwise it seemed like he was still alive. I watched as Sue put her hands over his and leaned to kiss his forehead.

By that time I was crying too.

"You're in Heaven now Frank with God," I told him.

"I'm glad you didn't suffer Frank and I hope you are at peace now," Gordon said, as he held my hand.

Sue turned and started to sob.

"What will I do?"

"Don't worry about anything right now, Sue. Gordon and I will make all the arrangements for you. I'll call Audrey right now and let her know."

Audrey, Sue's daughter, was married to Bob. They had two children and a busy lifestyle. Audrey was an only child and close to her father.

"This will hit her hard." Sue said out loud what I was thinking.

CHAPTER 62

PONY AND PUPPY RACES

1950s
DOT

I was sitting in the living room watching television when Dad walked in.

"I've got tickets to the Bruins game this Saturday. You want to go with me, Dot?"

"Yeah, sure Dad, I love the Bruins."

The truth was that I liked the Bruins, but I loved going with Dad. I'd listen to him yell if they scored a goal and watch him jump up and down. A few times I thought he would end up in a fray on the ice at Boston Garden.

Dad always got us tickets to the circus and ice follies too. No matter how busy he was with work, he found time for us children. Sometimes Ma would come with us, but she knew it was important for us to bond with Dad.

Neither of our parents drank. Dad got ulcers about the time that Priscilla was born and gave up alcohol almost entirely. Mom had no capacity for drink and only had one glass of champagne, usually on New Year's Eve to celebrate their anniversary. I can see her now, sitting in our living room sipping a glass of bubbly in the wing chair.

What Dad really enjoyed were the "Pony and Puppy" races as he called his horse and dog racing vices. When I was younger my best friend Sheila and I popped open his trunk one day. We were looking for a hammer, I can't remember why we needed a hammer, but when we popped open the trunk there were stacks and stacks of ticket stubs from the racetrack.

Then we got this great idea and started adding them up to see how much money he spent on gambling. We were having a good old time until Dad walked in and caught us.

"Dot! Close that trunk now!" He yelled at us, and then he made us promise not to tell Mom.

The other memorable occasion was the day I got my driver's license. Dad let me drive his red Ford pick-up truck. I was so proud to think he trusted me with his truck.

CHAPTER 63

THE TOTEM POLE BALLROOM

1958
DOT'S STORY

My parents were active in the Episcopal Church. They were raised in a very spiritual manner growing up in Newfoundland. They were served religion for breakfast, lunch, and dinner. Although my parents lived in America now they were still strict and raised us to attend church on Sundays. But they also encouraged us to be friendly and meet new people. I never needed encouraging for that.

The Totem Pole Ballroom was a popular dance hall. It was formerly part of Norumbega Park and was located near the Auburndale-on-the-Charles amusement park on the Charles River.

I sat around the kitchen table eating breakfast with my parents one morning. "I met a nice man while I was dancing at the Totem Pole last night."

"Tell us about him, Dot." I could see the curiosity in my mother's eyes.

"Well, he's from Waltham, he's a postman. Tom Noonan is his name. Ruthie's boyfriend, Danny, works at the post office with him. Well, we were all dancing the jitterbug and he asked me to dance. He can't dance at all, Ma! Stepped on my feet a couple of times, but so what?"

"Let's meet him sometime, Dot. You have a look that says he might be the one. But, you hardly know him, so don't be too hasty."

"I'm not, Ma, I like him well enough. My sisters are always calling me an old maid, but I'm just waiting for the right guy."

We dated for several months, and then Tom proposed. Tom asked my father for my hand in marriage, and he agreed.

"He seems like a nice enough fella. Seems smart," Dad said.

What I hadn't told my parents was that Tom was Catholic. I knew that Catholics marrying into the Protestant faith and vice versa was considered a "mixed marriage."

Mixed marriages were an emotion-charged issue then and way before the 1950s. I would marry in the Catholic Church, because Tom couldn't get married in the Episcopal Church without special dispensation from the Catholic Church. Although I agreed to get married at his church, I had no intention of converting to Catholicism.

Dad was livid when I broke the news.

"I'm not taking her down the aisle of a Catholic church," he ranted at my mother. "Tom should be willing to marry her in our church and that's final!"

My mother supported me, God bless her. I heard them arguing behind closed doors.

"Gordon, she's your daughter. It will break her heart if you don't walk her down the aisle."

"I just can't do it."

"Dot won't forgive you."

"Listen, I'll pay for the wedding. I'll be very civil to everyone, but I won't walk her down the aisle."

I ran down the stairs and slammed out the back door, tears streaming down my face. I was crying, but I was angry.

Ma was correct. I never did forgive him. I asked my brother Jim to walk me down the aisle. We tied the knot in September 1958. We held the reception at Monticello's in Framingham, and it was lovely. I never forgot that Dad refused to give me away. I was truly heartbroken. Later on my father regretted that decision, but by then it was too late.

CHAPTER 64

THE MOVIE CAMERA

1958
GLADYS

Gordon bought a 16 mm Bell and Howell movie camera. It became his new pride and joy. He nearly drove us off the road several times taking movies while driving.

Then one day, Gordon sprang a surprise on me.

"Glad, I know you love summers at the cottage, but this year I'd like to do something special for you. Let's take a few weeks this summer and visit our families down home. It's been awhile. We can drive up to Sydney, Nova Scotia, catch the ferry to Port aux Basques, and then drive to Twillingate. What do you think?"

Twillingate, the sound of that name was magical. Fond memories flooded back to me. I didn't hesitate to agree.

"Yes, I'd love to do that. I'd like to see Hilda and Pete. I haven't been home since Father died. Priscilla's never met any of her cousins or her aunts and uncles, and we can visit Heart's Delight."

"The kids can take an extra-long vacation at the cottage while we're gone, and that will make everyone happy."

We reserved our passage and I started packing. In the early years when we were poor, the children and I wore a lot of hand-me-downs and I always packed sparingly if we had to go on a trip. Now, I could buy all the clothes I wanted. And petite, I still had my petite figure.

I loved matching outfits, color-coordinated with shoes and purses. A pair of gloves for church and a hat would do. As I loaded my luggage into the oversized trunk of the Pontiac

Bonneville, Gordon gasped.

"Jeez, Glad! We're going for three weeks not a year!"

"I won't have my washer or the dry cleaners, so I'll need all of this and so will you and Priscilla."

On a warm summer day in July 1958, we left Dot to check on the house and off we went. We crossed into Nova Scotia and were greeted at the welcome center by men dressed in kilts and playing bagpipes. We drove the car onto the ferry and went to our cabin. I wasn't looking forward to any rough seas; especially after my harrowing experiences on the ferry the first time I met Gordon. It would be about an eight-hour voyage before we disembarked.

Priscilla wandered around the ship and then sat in the deck chairs with us. We sailed early, the sun was out and the seas calm, with a gentle easterly breeze. Gordon hoped we could drive as far as Corner Brook where his nephew and wife, Wilf and Susie Bishop, lived. We had planned an overnight visit.

It was a long trip, but when we finally arrived, we were welcomed with open arms, good food, and clean beds. We sat late into the night reminiscing; Wilf put a bottle of Screech rum on the table. "Remember this, Gordon?"

Gordon laughed. "Oh Boyo, do I ever!"

I watched as he placed his hand over the top of his glass when all of a sudden we heard a scream. Priscilla was out of bed standing at the top of the stairs crying.

She insisted she saw a ghost in her bedroom. After a vivid description of the "ghost," Susie admitted to us that a lady had died many years ago in the house. We told Priscilla it was a good ghost and reluctantly, she went to bed.

In the morning we enjoyed a hearty Newfie breakfast of porridge, codfish, and brewis, a hardtack that always reminded me of dog biscuits. We bid our farewells and took the rocky road on to Heart's Delight, Gordon's hometown. I had to remind him all over again.

"Gordon, for the love of God pay attention or we'll drive straight into a ditch."

I was glad I didn't drive, there were deep trenches on either side of the road that were used in winter for snow, but they were also traps for inattentive drivers. We drove down the rocky, narrow lanes winding our way to the next destination.

"That movie camera will be the death of us," I warned.

Gordon whistled as he stuck the Bell and Howell movie camera out the window. He continued taking movies, as he drove one-handed through the rough terrain.

CHAPTER 65

PRISCILLA'S NEWFOUNDLAND TRIP

SUMMER 1958
PRISCILLA

Being the youngest child in a family of seven had its ups and downs. Most of my siblings were so much older than me that at times I felt like I had three or four sets of parents. But I can say honestly that they all loved me, and if they were jealous of the attention that my mother bestowed on me from time to time, they never let it show. Unless I started whining, even then they were usually empty threats.

When I was eleven years old my parents decided to take me to Newfoundland. I would miss the beach parties at Marion, but being eleven they usually sent me to bed before anything too interesting happened anyway. And I'm sure interesting things happened that my parents never found out about.

I survived the ferry crossing to Newfoundland but I felt pretty topsy-turvy. I disembarked and my legs began to buckle. Dad caught me by the elbow and straightened me out.

"You've got to get your sea legs, Priscilla." What a funny expression I thought and why didn't I get my "sea legs" when we were on the ferry?

The villages in Newfoundland were set either directly on the shoreline or across the road from the shore. The streets were lined with clapboard houses and rocky beaches. Tall whale ribs served as arched entryways along the picket fences, fronting the walkway to each home.

Dad pulled over to a whaling factory to get pictures. He was infatuated with his Bell and Howell movie camera and took photos and moving pictures of everything. He videoed the long belts that dragged the strips of thick black whale skin. It reminded me of tire treads. I was pretty sad when Dad explained that this was the Newfoundlanders way of survival.

"Every part of the whale is used. Nothing wasted. The oil, the meat, the skin, and the bones are all processed. Whale oil is precious to their livelihood."

"The meat is sent to mink farms, and the skins from the mink are used for those fancy fur coats in the States."

I understood what he told me, but it made me sad. We drove along the coast for a while, and in the distance I saw a large iceberg floating on the horizon. Ma said that even in the summer you could see icebergs.

In the cove the fishermen were working with gaffs. The water was red with blood as the fishermen herded several pilot whales near the shore. I heard the whales' screams. Dad filmed it with his movie camera. They were killing the whales; it upset me so much I asked my father to leave.

"Okay, Pris, we'll keep driving."

My mother told me not to cry. It was dark by the time we reached Heart's Delight, my father's hometown.

I couldn't believe it, there were ponies walking along the roads and sheep wandering on the shoulder. We parked in one of the lanes and Dad's family, my family, circled the car. They lived in a 150 year-old house and except for a few additions, it appeared much the same as the original family photo from 1909 that was hanging in our house.

They even brought in our luggage for us. Mom had bought gifts for everyone and as we gathered in the kitchen, the smell of fresh home-baked bread wafted around the room.

Dad's sister Eva was still running the household. Her hair was in plaits and pinned up in circlets around her ears like a farm girl, just like Mom described her. She gave us all big hugs.

"My, my, it's so good to see you here, loves."

Uncle Am sat in a rocker beside the woodstove. This is the first time I've met them. He looks really old to me.

Eva and Ambrose's son Gordon was named after my father. Gordon and his wife Mary would have ten children. Ten! The kids are all around us with hugs and smiles. They are curious about me, but I'm too shy to say much.

In the kitchen is a long wooden table with benches. We gather around and everyone is talking at the same time. In the corner is a day bed. The wood stove is black but the chrome is shiny. A wooden barrel sits to one side of the stove. This is where they keep that delicious smelling homemade bread I'm told.

"Tea!! Get the kettle on!" Aunt Eva orders Mary.

Out came homemade cakes, biscuits, sugar, tinned milk, and hot tea.

CHAPTER 66

ST. JOHN'S TO TWILLINGATE

1958
GLADYS

We headed towards St. John's, the capital, with Priscilla in the back seat. We were about an hour's drive from Heart's Delight, and were looking forward to our visit with Gordon's relatives.

St. John's was the oldest British settlement in North

America. The landlocked harbor could only be approached through a long, narrow channel, protected by the high hills on which the city was built.

Gordon has a sister named Priscilla (my daughter's namesake); she is actually Gordon's half-sister from his mother's first marriage. His mother's first husband died young.

Priscilla's son Bill married Marian. They have three children. Bob and Christine live in the house on Black Drive in St. John's where we're headed. Winston their other son is living with his Uncle Wilf and Aunt Susie in Corner Brook.

Jen and Lena Minnie, both spinsters, are Priscilla's other adult children, and they live there also.

They're good people, but overly protective. Jen has every ailment known to man and she's always overdressed to ward off colds. She welcomed us warmly, she's a kind, loving, and thoughtful person.

Lena Minnie is a petite lady; her eyes are unusually small. She looks different, unusual, and Gordon whispers to me that some people think she is physically impaired, but Lena is not going to allow the pampering to keep her in the house. She is dressed in her Salvation Army outfit and off to do good works.

There is a regatta at Boering Park this weekend, and we've decided we'll just take this whole germ-paranoid family with us. The day is sunny and bright, no chill in the air, and a gentle breeze ripples the water. We set out a picnic lunch on the grass and watch the boat races.

It was here in St. John's on my journey to America that I first met Gordon. I have many fond memories when I think back to that day so long ago.

We didn't return to Heart's Delight until late that evening, and we drove carefully to avoid the moose, stray ponies, and grazing sheep that roamed close to the road.

Our vacation flew by. I called my sister Hilda to arrange our upcoming visit to Twillingate. Captain Peter Troake, her husband will be on shore leave for a few days, so it's best that we go straight away. We drive along the coast on our way to Twillingate.

The beautiful but remote locations of Newfoundland's coastal towns came with the unfortunate price of inaccessibility. This presented a number of challenges including unavailable healthcare and education. The only form of transportation to and from these towns was by boat, which made the trip into town to see a doctor inconvenient, expensive, and difficult. Hilda's husband Pete is the captain of the MV Christmas Seal, a famous medical ship. It's fitted out to provide chest X-rays, and carry out vaccinations, test and treat tuberculosis and polio, and test for diabetes.

Since 1950 the Christmas Seal traveled from village to village treating those with the disease. Pete himself had tuberculosis and encouraged patients who were reluctant to have x-rays as a preventative measure.

Captain Pete was often away at sea, leaving the raising of their three children up to my sister Hilda. She was up to the challenge. A strong healthy woman, Hilda killed the chickens, milked the cows, worked the garden, and raised three kids. Their son, Jack, a fisherman, is married and lives in the home I grew up in, located right next to Hilda and Pete's house. Hilda's home is a gorgeous two-story Victorian built in the late 1880s. She finally got her wish and married a famous Captain.

I couldn't wait to see them. The village had changed, there were more houses and shops now. Twillingate seemed a hub of activity, compared to the old days. Ocean-going vessels traveled to all parts of the world. There was an atmosphere of excitement, as we watched the boats navigate the harbor as fishermen brought in their catch.

We headed up to Hilda's house. She stood at the doorstep

waiting for us, full of hugs and kisses.

"Good Lord, it's so good to see you!"

"Yes! It's been too long, sis."

Hilda was prepared for us, it was noon and she had a pot of tea and a hearty lunch laid out. The kitchen was bright and sunny, with a large woodstove. I loved her dining room the most. A local artist had painted the walls in oils. There was a scenic treescape with the ocean and sailing ships in the distance.

Hilda has lived on the island all her life. She sat in the middle of the sofa, a hand knit sweater over her shoulders. Unlike my sisters and me, Hilda has a perfectly round face, thick wavy hair gone gray; she is square-built and sturdy, and she talked on as if she were the only one with something important to say.

After lunch we got the grand tour of the house and of course everything was immaculate. Elizabeth and Doreen, her daughters, invited Priscilla to walk around the village and meet their friends and distant cousins. Elizabeth looked more like Hilda, dark hair and round face. Doreen had red hair and favored my father, I thought.

Pete and Gordon enjoyed each other's stories. It was nice and reminded me that storytelling was an integral part of Newfoundland life. Hilda and I had a cup of tea while she filled me in on everything that had happened on the island since I was there last, which was quite a lot.

It's been a heartwarming journey. I enjoyed spending time with my sister and sharing our memories. Sadly it's time to return to Heart's Delight, pack and then head back home to the States. I enjoyed the trip but I was looking forward to being at the Cape with my family next year.

CHAPTER 67

FRANNIE & BILL

1958-1959
GLADYS

"Germany was great, but I had trouble with the language," Bill laughed with that distinct Boston accent and said, "Must have been my 'BAHSton' accent."

The Army had been good for him, and there had been no active duty, really a blessing I thought.

"Bill, you can stay here as long as you want. Your old room on the porch is ready for you."

"That's great, Ma, thanks." He planted a big kiss on my head and I was thrilled.

"I went down to Mount Auburn Cemetery this week, they're hiring."

"The cemetery! Do you really want to work there?" I was surprised.

"Why not, Mom, it's a job. I just hope it won't freak me out too much."

Bill worked there for six months and decided working at the shop would be better. No surprise there.

"I'm taking my friend, Frannie, to her high school prom. She's a nice girl. You'll like her."

"Bring her by tonight before the prom. We would love to meet her."

As promised, they stopped by that evening. They both looked so nice. Frannie was a pretty dark-haired girl and extremely friendly. Gordon liked her. I thought it might be a good match, but it was way too early to tell.

They were married in January of 1959. They rented an

apartment in Somerville on the third floor. It was a hike, at least for me, to go up and down the stairs, but they were young and that's what they could afford.

Bill joined up with his father in the business. He and his brother Gordon looked at potential jobs and wrote estimates. He got his feet wet in rigging and then moved on to heavy machinery. His brother Jim worked there too, but Jim kept to his own group with Uncle Bill and his cousin Bob.

All our grown children were married now. The years have sped by.

The Primmer family home
in Twillingate

Heber Primmer
on the hunt

Gladys with her Marseille wave
for her wedding

Peter and Hilda Troake at
their home in Twillingate

Captain Troake as commander
of the MV Christmas Seal

Gladys at home
on Chetwynd Road

Gordon with a cow
for Mission to Mexico

1960s

CHAPTER 68

GRANDCHILDREN

1960s
GLADYS

We ushered in a New Year with party horns and noisemakers as we said farewell to the decade. It was 1960 and the world was changing rapidly. Our family numbers were growing significantly. I did a rundown as I sat at the kitchen table with Gordon one Sunday morning later that year.

"Gordon, our family is growing by leaps and bounds."

"Yes, Gladys." I could tell right then and there he wasn't really listening but I continued my count down.

"First, Jim and Anna, plus the kids Michael, Neal, Paul, Donna, and Gordon."

"Yes, dear."

I smiled; Gordon was deep in the horseracing results.

"Then there's Uldine and Howie. That's another six," I counted them off on my fingers: Kathryn, Wendy, Earl, Brian, Sandra, and Laura. "Of course we can't forget Louise."

"No, dear." Gordon turned the page.

"So there's Louise and Fred's three, David, Steven, and Elizabeth. Then Gordon and Pearl with Kirby. Then there's Bill and Frannie's Linda, and last but not least there's Dot and Tom. Of course they haven't started a family yet."

"No, dear."

A full house, sixteen and counting. I was in my element!

I got up and took the newspaper. "Gordon, are you listening to a word I've said?"

All the kids loved going to the cottage in the summer, then

Thanksgiving was a major event at the Harnum household, and Christmas shopping and decorations started early for all the grandchildren.

1960 would be our last Thanksgiving on Chetwynd Road and the dining room overflowed with family. The children sat around card tables that we set up for them in the living room. It was also the year that several of us got ptomaine poisoning.

I was always so careful and clean but somehow it happened. Poor Pearl, she fell sick with ptomaine poisoning and went to the hospital. They gave her some medication and thank goodness she had a full recovery. I felt terrible; it was her first Thanksgiving with the family. I knew it was silly, but I worried it would be her last Thanksgiving dinner with us. She probably thought I tried to poison her.

In the coming years Jim and Anna had two more sons, Daniel and Gary. Louise and Fred had one more son, Frederick. Gordon had two more sons, Douglas and Keith. Dot had Thomas and Deborah. Bill had two sons, William and Phillip, and another girl, Jill.

CHAPTER 69

THE MOVE TO BELMONT

1961
GLADYS

Gordon and I sold the home on Chetwynd Road in Cambridge to our son Bill and his wife Fran. We were happy for them and they were very happy to have a home of their own.

It took us several months to build our new home at 61 Glenn Road in Belmont. There were no other homes on that road at the time. The land belonged to a vegetable farm called Sergi's Farm. It was very convenient; I just walked across the street to buy fresh vegetables at the stand. It was only a short walk from the bus line, just perfect for me. I never did get my driver's license. I was too nervous.

It was an exciting move for Gordon and me, but not for Priscilla. She was in her first year of high school and had grown up with all her friends in Cambridge. She could continue there for one more year, but after that she would need to transfer to Belmont. That first year many of her friends took the MBTA bus and came to visit her after school.

Her sisters encouraged her to go to Belmont High - they had better teachers, and smaller classrooms, and it was in a more affluent town. She begged us to pay tuition to stay another year in Cambridge. Priscilla could take the MBTA to Harvard Square to finish off the year at Cambridge High and Latin. We agreed reluctantly.

Our new home had everything I wished for. I had it painted all in white. There were three bedrooms, a den, two and a half baths, hardwood floors, and a wood-burning fireplace, which we never used. We had a full basement with a two-car garage underneath. We paid cash of course - after living through the Depression, we decided any personal purchases would always be paid in cash.

The new house had lots of room for family at Thanksgiving and Christmas. Our friends and family visited often. It was a revolving door of people and everyone was welcome.

Heber and Ethel Crocker lived behind us on the cul de sac. Andy Crocker and his wife and son lived in Belmont. They were all Newfoundlanders. Their son became friends with Priscilla when she finally started at Belmont High.

We hosted lots of dinner parties and card games with our Newfoundland friends. I loved to shop, and we could finally afford it. Gordon put money in the checking account every week, and I never balanced the checkbook, ever. There was always enough there. Mind you, I wasn't wasteful or extravagant but there were always things to buy for the new house and birthday and Christmas presents for the grandkids. Besides, a trip to the city or Jordan Marsh once a week made me happy. I took the bus at the corner and got on the train to Boston in Harvard Square.

SUE

Sue moved in with us the following year. She was retired and widowed now. We welcomed her with open arms. We all got along well with her, and Sue and Priscilla loved each other. Gordon would arrive home from work, and he usually bought a pastry for dessert. He boasted how lucky he was, he loved sweets and kept his figure. Sue was casual and would come to the dinner table in a housecoat and slippers. I enjoyed cooking and Sue didn't mind cleaning up. One thing we all had in common, we liked to eat. None of us were ever fat, but we ate often.

Breakfast usually consisted of cream of wheat with toast and jam. If we were home Sue and I ate crackers and cheese around ten, and a light lunch around one. Supper was at six, and we watched the 11:00 p. m. evening news accompanied by crackers or biscuits with tea. We usually played a few hands of cards, Hearts or Gin Rummy, before retiring to bed.

I liked to keep busy, so in my spare time I ran the church thrift shop. I also organized church suppers and the Penny and Rummage sales. Gordon was on the vestry and contributed not only money but also his good judgment and his time. St. James's Church was very much a part of our lives.

Children watching a house being towed from Fox Island. August 1961.

(National Archives of Canada, PA-154123 www.collectionscanada.gc.ca) used with permission

Mr. Malcolm Rogers' house moored to the shore awaits high tide, during relocation
from Fox Island to Flat Island. August 1961

CHAPTER 70

RESETTLEMENT

1950s to 1970s

Once bustling with a thriving fishing industry, homes, outbuildings, and wharves lay silent throughout most of the outports.

From the mid 1950s until the 1970s, the Newfoundland government closed 250 coastal outports. When Joseph Smallwood, the Premier, saw that the fisheries were no longer thriving because of foreign overfishing, he went to the small communities and said, "If the majority of you want to move to a larger community, we will give each of you $2,000. But after you move, you can't go back."[1]

Thousands of people, mostly fishermen, were uprooted from their homes and relocated to larger villages or towns. The idea was to centralize isolated communities scattered along the coast of Newfoundland.

The government believed this would provide better education, health care, roads, and electricity, and for some it did. It was also expected to create jobs outside of the fisheries, one of the primary sources of income for Newfoundlanders.

Most fishermen never saw that much money in a lifetime. Many people moved to St. John's. Not all the houses were relocated. Many that were left were abandoned, torn down, or fell apart. Once the communities were moved, the government was gone.

Newfoundlanders were left in an unknown location having left their homes, family, their livelihood, and a support network. Some families had left signs on their front door "Use but please

Do Not Abuse!" Some families intended to return in the spring to prepare to move their houses across the bay. Many of those that returned home the following season found their homes ransacked. Outbuildings were broken into and their fishing gear, their very livelihood, stolen.

Unlike communities that had succumbed to the temptation to take the money and resettle on the main, the community of Twillingate resisted. It was a devastating time, and no wonder many Newfoundlanders hung the Canadian flag upside down.

[1]*Excerpts from Larry Hahn, http://www.terroirsymposium.com/resettlement/, used with permission.*

CHAPTER 71

SANDWICH

1959-1966
GLADYS

I was so glad we had built the cottage in Marion, and then Heber and Fannie bought a cottage in Sandwich, the oldest town on Cape Cod and not too far from us. We were so happy they would be close. It was a great time, filled with laughter whenever we visited.

I sat at the kitchen table and Fannie had a big grin and looked about to burst into laughter as if she had the best joke in town.

"What is it, Fannie, what's so funny?" She burst out in a gale of giggles.

She laughed so hard, soon I was laughing with her, but I had no idea why. She was just always happy!

Heber and Fannie enjoyed fishing on nearby Cape Cod Canal, a seven-mile waterway for freighters, sailing ships, and yachts to cut across the Cape. Fannie wore bib overalls and a Greek captain's hat. Taller and stockier than Heber, they made a comical pair. Fannie loved to cook and we were guaranteed a hearty meal and a very delicious but fattening dessert.

They never had children, although they would have made the best parents. Instead they enjoyed each other as best friends and were a happily married couple. Heber was an accomplished carpenter, and his specialty was bowling alleys. The alleys were designed to be perfectly level.

Both of them were born in Twillingate and stayed connected to family and friends there. They enjoyed keeping up with the stories of the island villagers. They kept their multi-family home in East Cambridge for income and maintained an apartment there when they were not summering in Sandwich.

In January 1966 Fannie succumbed to a heart attack. Heber was lost without her.

Photo on page 173
(1927, l to r) Gladys Primmer, Fannie Tucker Primmer, Susannah Primmer Jenkins

CHAPTER 72

HOWIE

1962
GLADYS

We were settled in our new home, and Priscilla was back in school. We received a call from a terrified Uldine.

"Ma, Howie is bleeding. He's on the sofa waiting for an ambulance. It's bad, Dad, please meet us at the Choate Hospital."

While they waited for the ambulance, Howie gave Uldine instructions.

"There is plenty of insurance. Enough to pay off the house."

They had purchased a cape in Burlington almost two years before.

"The house is for the kids," he said. "Earl is too much for you to handle and you need to find a place, an institution that has kids like Earl."

Uldine listened quietly with tears streaming down her face as they waited what seemed like an eternity for the ambulance to arrive. Uldine accompanied him in the ambulance. Her neighbors watched the children.

Uldine waited while Howie was wheeled into surgery.

"Bleeding ulcers, it doesn't look good," the doctor told her.

"Oh God, Dad." She rushed to Gordon as he walked into the emergency room.

Gordon waited six hours with Uldine as they operated but they couldn't save him.

She returned home to her six children minus a husband, and with no father for her children.

CHAPTER 73

BELMONT HIGH

1963
GLADYS

Priscilla agreed to finish high school at Belmont High. I think she felt pressured not to seem spoiled and make us pay tuition for school again. Don't get me wrong, we didn't mind paying tuition at all, but we thought she would be fine at Belmont. Boy, were we wrong. She seemed so confident on the outside, but on the inside she was a bit insecure and would be quiet if she didn't feel comfortable in a group conversation.

She knew no one at Belmont and found it difficult to fit in with the new group of kids. She eventually made friends but they were not very close friends. She needed friends who she could trust and bond with.

To make matters worse, although we never thought about it that way, Gordon bought her a new car. He bought it because I never drove or had a license, and it seemed like a good idea at the time. He was so busy with work and about to move the business, he thought that Priscilla could drive me around. Well, she did, but she also drove the car to school every day.

One of the few girls that had a car, the boys harassed her for rides. The boys would jump in the car when she stopped at Belmont Center, filling twelve kids at a time into her car, and they wouldn't get out. They thought it was funny, a big joke.

The police spotted the commotion one day and cited her for overloading the car. One time the boys soaped her car windows on the inside when she left the vent window unlocked.

We didn't know what was going on. She kept it to herself and spent more time in Harvard Square visiting her old friends.

CHAPTER 74

THE GAS EXPLOSION

1963 WOBURN
GLADYS

It was a cold January morning when Sue's daughter Audrey, her husband Bob and their three children, Janet, Robert, and Donald walked through our front door with literally nothing but the clothes on their backs.

"Aunt Gladys, we've lost our home," Audrey said.

Bob had gotten up early that morning and went down into their basement to get his toolbox, when he smelled gas. He yelled for his family.

"GET UP!! Run!! Run out the house. Right now!!!!!"

Sensing the urgency in his shouts, the kids obeyed and ran across the road. They stood there in the chill of a new day and watched as their home exploded in front of their very eyes. There was nothing left. Not a single picture, not so much as a spoon.

The angels along with their fast acting dad were watching over them that day, otherwise they would have all been blown to bits. There was insurance on the house and the neighborhood raised money to help replace what they had lost. Most importantly, they were alive. I called my daughters and cousins, and we dug out as many spare family photos as we could find and gave them to Audrey and Bob.

Photographs are the precious records of our lives, and really that was their greatest loss. Furniture and dishes and clothes would all be replaced in time.

CHAPTER 75

EARL GOES TO BELCHERTOWN

1964
GLADYS

Despite the doctor's poor prognosis Earl continued to grow and develop. Uldine abided by her late husband's wishes, and had researched places to send Earl. Most of them were institutions for Cerebral Palsy, Downs Syndrome, and various forms of retardation. It was a heartbreaking decision but it was impossible for her to care for him and five children as well.

Earl had developed a strong upper body but he could still not walk properly and he could only utter a few words. Uldine would fill a dishpan with detergent soap and plastic dishes for him to wash. He would pull himself up to the sink, and happily wash the plastic dishes over and over again. It also kept his hands clean from crawling around on the floor. He was not violent, but he could throw things and he had occasional seizures. Institutionalization seemed the only answer at the time. Poor Uldine, she was bent over from lifting him.

An institution in Belchertown accepted him. A few hours away, it contained a series of brick buildings and the occupants were of every type of disability. Once a month Uldine and I would drive the two hours and take Earl out to lunch. It was a sad place, filled with moaning and yelling. Earl would always be dressed in clean clothes and ready for his outing, and he was usually excited to see us. We hoped they took good care of him but we had no way of knowing for sure. We checked him for bruises and marks and found none.

We usually had lunch at the closest restaurant. Belchertown was small, making a limited selection of restaurants. Excited once we got to the restaurant, Earl would get loud and of course he had to be hand fed. Most diners had compassion and didn't make a fuss.

But, every once in a while, someone would complain. I tried to protect my Uldine and Earl from their stares and jeers. I might be small, but I would lay right into them.

"Stop staring," I raised my voice. "There, but for the Grace of God go you or me! What kind of person are you? You don't know what life will bring you so you better not embarrass yourself."

I'm sure I just embarrassed myself mostly, but people backed off, ate quickly, and left.

Good riddance, I thought.

Earl was there for twenty years; then they closed it down. Eventually all institutions like Belchertown were closed down. They were replaced with group homes instead, and Earl was assigned to a wonderful home in Lexington, the next town from us in Belmont.

His caregivers were truly angels and they really cared for Earl. There were only eight patients in the house and they called them "residents." They took them on outings, and most of the residents seemed to be happy. We were able to see Earl more often and he was able to attend family gatherings.

CHAPTER 76

NEWFOUNDLAND BY VW BUS

SUMMER 1964
LOUISE

"Mom, Fred and I are taking all the kids in the Volkswagen bus to Newfoundland. Does Priscilla want to come with us?"

"Yes!" Priscilla bobbed her head up and down enthusiastically.

Fred and I loved to travel and Priscilla spent a lot of time with our family. We had moved into Fred's family's rather antique farmhouse in Acton. It was a typical New England style home with a large attached barn. Not very modern but it had character and had been Fred's parents' home before they died.

His brother Joe lived in the farmhouse before with his wife and (eventually) nine kids. There was lots of acreage and it had been divided between Fred's siblings. Joe built a cape on part of the allotted land next to the farmhouse, leaving it vacant and available until we could build across Newtown Road on our allotment.

Fred's older sister Genevieve had a home across the road and had a small beauty parlor in her basement. She had a daughter and son, slightly older and slightly younger than Priscilla. We were one big happy family of Hryniewichs.

While our house was being constructed, a trip to Newfoundland sounded like a great adventure. We drove off, the bus loaded with camping gear and boxes of canned goods. As we drove along the kids could look out the windows and the skylight. We camped at Arcadia Park for a night on the way to the ferry to Newfoundland. Arcadia National Park has red mud at the riverbank and a rocky shoreline at the coast.

Once we landed on the island of Newfoundland, the rain started. We were prepared - we had packed galoshes, umbrellas, and rainwear. The roads were rocky, narrow, and uneven, and edged with snow ditches.

Not long into the journey the heavy rain created deep slippery ruts in the road and the VW bus tossed and turned until it lost its balance and landed in a snow ditch leaning on its right side. Canned goods flew out of the boxes narrowly missing everyone.

"Is everyone okay back there?" I shouted.

"Yes, Mom!" they said in unison, enjoying it a little too much. "We're all fine. The cans just missed us."

"What a mess!" Priscilla said.

"We'll have to sleep here for the night. There's hardly a soul around," Fred said. "Hopefully someone will see us in the morning and tow us out."

Not long after that came a tap on the muddied windows. A man shouted, "Are ye there by chance or by choice?"

"By chance," Fred shouted.

"Yer not hurt are ye?"

"No, we're all fine," Fred said as he rolled down the window.

"Well, if ye can last the night I'll have some fellers come a get ye out in the morning."

Sure enough the next morning five or six men came with an old truck and tied ropes to the front and dragged the bus along, while three men pushed it upright with Fred. The rest of us stood on the road in the rain and watched.

"You're a godsend, thank you. What do we owe you? We're so grateful."

"Nay, not a copper. Just glad yer fine and yer car runs. Where are ye off to?"

"Heart's Delight where my father was born."

"Oh then, be off with ye to see yer kin."

The Salvation Army Building

In 1968 Fred and I returned to visit Twillingate and Heart's Delight. We bought the old Salvation Army Building for two thousand dollars. A small square building used for meetings with a bath and a makeshift kitchen, it was perfect for short vacations. It faced Trinity Bay with an unobstructed view.

CHAPTER 77

UNA MISIÓN A MÉXICO
&
THE STETSON HAT

1964
GORDON

I was quite involved in supporting our local church. Gladys and I attended St. James's Episcopal Church in Cambridge. Gladys was an active member and leader in organizing many of the church functions and fundraisers. She supported my involvement in the church too.

It was 1964, the Civil Rights Act had been signed into law. It was supposed to eliminate discrimination on the basis of race and gender in the workplace. It was an admirable move, but I always judged a man or a woman by their work ethic. I worked hard and expected my family and employees to do the same.

Gladys and I were at Sunday service when the Reverend Way stopped us on our way out to chat.

"Gordon, how would you like to go to Mexico with me?"

"Mexico?" I asked, thinking I hadn't heard him correctly.

"Yes, you and I have been chosen to take 'Living Gifts' to Mexico."

"Really, what is that, tell me a little more."

"We will fly into San Antonio, Texas. Transport for some forty livestock animals to cross the border into Mexico has been arranged. You and I get the blessing of delivering them into the interior of Mexico to twenty needy families who have biblically cast their lots in a lottery to receive one of our 'Living Gifts,' a life-saving animal."

"You're in? Right, Gordon?"

Reverend Way really wanted me to go, and he added one more thing.

"God has chosen us to do this."

I couldn't refuse Reverend Way. I smiled. "Yes! I'm in."

Three truckloads filled with forty-eight animals left Groton, Massachusetts under heavy snowfall and arrived at the Mexican border two days later.

Gladys, always nervous about travel, agreed I should go and promised to pray for our safe return.

Reverend Way and I were at the border when the trucks arrived. There the awaiting animals, cows, chickens, and goats were transferred to smaller trucks and driven from village to village over the washed out roads.

The pastor and I returned the next day. I was all choked up as I told Gladys what an unforgettable experience to see the joy on people's faces as the trucks arrived in the center of their remote villages with the live gifts.

I had a full heart, but Gladys said, "What on earth is that on your head?"

It was a large tan Stetson cowboy hat.

"It's my new hat, Glad. I can wear it when it snows. Ha-ha!" And I did.

CHAPTER 78

CONFESSIONAL

1965
PRISCILLA

Pen in hand I stared at the blank page. How do I tell this story? It's been hidden away in my memory for so many years. It's always been part of my inherent nature and upbringing to want to please. I pleased my family, my teachers, and my friends. I could go without, if it meant helping a friend in need. That usually meant I never said "no."

In 1965 Dad bought me a green Studebaker Lark. The idea was I'd get a license and the Lark. In return, I would drive Mom around to the shops, and use it to drive to school. Dad was always too busy with work to drive us around. So naturally I agreed.

In some ways this "gift" became my downfall.

The new car made me stand out at school. I was new to Belmont High. Petite and attractive with long blonde hair, I instantly became a target for the high school boys. As a joke, or just to torment me, they would pile into my car and refuse to get out. I didn't want them there but I would agree to drive them somewhere in order to get rid of them.

It was late June and the weather warm. I'd been invited to a party in Central Square, a short drive from Harvard Square. It was a group of my old Cambridge friends, and I looked forward to going. The party was in full swing by the time I got there.

I didn't drink much; to be honest I couldn't hold more than one drink. But I was in a good mood and ready to party with my friends.

I enjoyed the evening and camaraderie, but it was getting

late, and I had a twenty-minute drive home to Belmont. I promised my parents I would be home by 11:30 p.m. A boy I knew from Cambridge High asked for a ride. It became a turning point in my life.

We were on our way back from Central Square when he asked me to drive down an alley, a "shortcut" he called it. Along with being young and innocent, I was always agreeable, so I turned off into the alley. It never even occurred to me that the alley wasn't a shortcut.

I never thought he would forcibly violate me. How could I be so naïve? I couldn't fight him off. I drove home in a puddle of tears. I couldn't stop crying. I knew it wasn't my fault, but I was filled with shame.

I told no one, and never mentioned his name again. But by then it was too late - I was already carrying the truth. My friend Dale went with me to a special doctor. I felt overwhelmed with guilt, but I did it. I ended up in the Cambridge City Hospital for an emergency D and C. My parents, God bless them, were so understanding, they were just grateful that I was alive.

ENTER LARRY

The incident changed the course of my life. My parents put it behind them and celebrated that I had been accepted at New York School of Design and the University of Massachusetts at Amherst.

But with all that going for me, plus a rosy career future, I decided to get married. I married Dale's ex-boyfriend Larry. He had come to visit me during my hospital stay. He was kind to me and I was at a low point in my life.

Larry had just finished his tour of duty in the Navy. Divorced with two sons, I found him attractive with his black-brown eyes. He looked just like James Dean. He was a diesel mechanic and I was strong willed and impulsive back then. I was at my brother Bill and Frannie's house babysitting my nieces and nephews when he asked me to marry him. It wasn't the most romantic proposal, but I agreed immediately.

My parents were astonished. They did everything they could to dissuade me, even going so far as to call his ex-wife. They handed the phone to me and she tried to discourage me too. Stubborn, I couldn't be reasoned with. I thought I could stand up for myself. But the true reason I married was that I felt damaged and lucky to have someone who wanted me.

My parents were very disappointed. Mom wanted a wedding for her last daughter. I didn't really want a wedding but out of guilt I agreed. I felt like I had already caused them pain and embarrassment.

And just like that, Larry and I went to my prom, I graduated high school, and we got married.

St. James's Episcopal Church wouldn't marry us because Larry was divorced. The United Methodist Church in Harvard Square would.

My parents paid for the reception at the popular Hotel Commander in Harvard Square. Larry's parents attended. They drove all the way from Ohio. His parents were very quiet and polite people. Larry's friends on the other hand were a rough crowd, loud, a bunch of drunks really. We honeymooned at his parents in Ohio so I could meet his family. They had five sons each five years apart. His ex-wife also lived in town and Larry wanted to see his sons. We went there and sat in her prim little living room. She and her boys stared at us from the other side of the room. She had two beautiful little boys, three and four years old.

Larry reached out to them and said, "I'm your father."

The older boy said, "My father is dead."

CHAPTER 79

KIMBERLY LOUISE FAIR

April 8, 1966
PRISCILLA

Barely eleven months after we married, Kimberly, my daughter, was born. Only six pounds, she had blue eyes and blond tufts for hair. She had all the best features of her father. She had a small perky nose, and ears that didn't stick out like mine. Kim, my own precious little baby girl, I adored her.

My parents came to see Kim.

"A babe with a babe," said my mother as she scooped Kim up into her arms. From that moment on, Kim became the light of my mother's life. I felt like she had replaced me with my own baby. Although there were many other grandchildren in our family, it was apparent that she favored tiny Kim.

One thing we had in common, Mom loved to shop. I'd visit her for the day and we'd drive to Belmont Center for a shopping spree at Peck and Peck for her, and Filenes for Kim and me. But she bought clothes mostly for Kim, darling outfits too expensive for me to afford. Occasionally Mom would buy one for me.

Larry and I bought a Campanelli slab home in Brockton. The Campanelli brothers were known for building large tracts of affordable single-family houses. Ours was a cookie cutter ranch on a busy road. I knew nothing about Brockton, but Larry had biker friends there. It was a very blue-collar neighborhood. I cashed out $500.00 from a small insurance policy my parents took out for me, and used it for our down payment. There were no underwriters or red tape - $500.00 cash and it was ours.

CHAPTER 80

THERE'S SOMETHING
ABOUT MARY

1966
PRISCILLA

A few months after we moved into the Brockton house I received a phone call from my friend Mary. I hadn't seen her in a couple of years.

"Priscilla, I just need a place to rest for a day, can I stay with you?"

"Of course, is everything alright?" I thought it was an odd request.

"Thank you so much, I've just had an abortion and I can't go home yet. My father would kill me."

Mary was beautiful in every way; she was thin and willowy with everything in just the right proportions. Blue eyes, long blond hair, and delicate hands, and perfect in every other way except she had a harelip. It was obvious but men fell in love with her anyway.

"I think it will be ok for a day or two," I said with caution. "I have a six-month-old baby girl. Did you know that?"

"No, I didn't, that's wonderful, Priscilla."

Soon after a new looking red Cadillac pulled into the driveway. A black man the size of a football player helped Mary out of the passenger seat. I wondered what was going on. It didn't seem to make sense, but I opened the door to them. Thank goodness Larry wasn't home.

Mary clutched her stomach. "You're pregnant too!" I exclaimed.

"I haven't lost it yet," she said. She introduced the man as having medical experience and said he would be back to pick her up. He handed me a bottle of Cherry Herring.

"Give this to her when the pain gets bad. Call me when it's over, I'll be back for her." The Cadillac backed out of the driveway. I started to panic.

"Mary, why didn't you tell me the truth? Oh my God! Why did I get involved in this?"

"Please, Priscilla, I need your help. I can't face this alone."

She was in labor and five months pregnant. I brought her into the extra bedroom and she lay on the daybed in pain. I had little Kim in a carrier in the other room. I kept checking on her. I prayed Mary didn't die. Then I prayed harder when she started screaming in pain. I put the bottle of Cherry Herring to her lips.

"Drink this, Mary!" I prayed she wouldn't die.

I feared the neighbors would call the police if they heard her screams. I kept thinking I would go to jail if she died. I walked Mary around the room and she lay down and it was soon over. The baby was dead, a horrible grey blue color. I think that maybe she was more than five months pregnant, because the baby looked perfectly formed. I called the man in the red Cadillac immediately, my hands shaking as I dialed.

"Please, come get Mary right away," I pleaded.

He must have been close by; it seemed only minutes before he arrived. He helped Mary and wrapped the baby in a towel.

"What will you do with the baby?"

He said, and I'll never forget it, "There are many babies buried along the 128."

Mary thanked me. I nodded. That was all I could do. I couldn't even look at her. How could she put me in such a predicament? No words came from my mouth.

I told Larry everything as soon as he came home. He was furious with me.

"She could have died and you would have faced arrest, and

what about Kim? What were you thinking, Priscilla?"

"What kind of friend would ask you to stay while she finished aborting a baby? Never speak to her again. Never be that stupid again."

The Brockton to Cambridge drive to work with the traffic on Route 128 became too much for Larry. I hated Brockton and every time I drove down the 128, the words of Mary's friend echoed in my mind.

"There are many babies buried along the 128."

I felt there was a bad karma in the house. We decided to move back to Somerville until we figured out where to go.

CHAPTER 81

SOLD!

1967
GLADYS

G. H. Harnum business thrived and eventually it needed a larger facility for all the trucks, equipment, and employees.

The Industrial Park in Wilmington was just such a place. It had plenty of land to park the trucks and equipment, plus a two-story office building with two huge garages for truck repairs, mechanics, and tools. Sadly we sold "The Shop." But Gordon as usual was always forward thinking.

The company bought another trucking business called Testa Trucking. Gordon added a crane service, Harco Crane Co. There were offices on the second floor for Gordon and our son young Gordon. They had a computer room, a lunchroom, and desk space for the accounting and billing person and a receptionist. Downstairs was Bill's office plus three offices for the dispatchers. A large percentage of the employees were family or friends of family. That sometimes caused trouble.

The company needed more land to store large equipment from job projects, mostly unwanted from the same projects and to be sold at a future date. Gordon purchased a parcel of land in New Hampshire and Jim was assigned to manage it. It was best for Jim to be separated from the main business. It kept the peace. Really, he was just not cut out to deal with clients. He had a negative, abrasive side to him at times.

CHAPTER 82

A TRIP TO NEWFOUNDLAND

1968
GLADYS

It was 1968 and G.H. Harnum was booming. Gordon suggested we go for a visit home.

"We'll only stay a month. The boys are doing a fine job here, but there's a lot going on. I can leave it a month, but not any longer than that. We've hired more men and bought more trucks. It's overwhelming. I need to be there, watching over what everyone is doing. Things get missed if someone is not minding the store as they say." Gordon raised his eyebrows, nodding his head to confirm his own insight.

"Fine, Gordon, I'll start packing."

Part of me didn't want to go. I loved our new cottage in Newfoundland and the stunning views overlooking Trinity Bay. But I still loved the beach cottage in Marion and would miss our time there this summer. Also, I wasn't looking forward to the long drive and the ferry ride to Newfoundland. Gordon was always looking at everything when he should be watching the road and I sighed, resigned to a long trip.

However my spirits lifted when Sue agreed to go on the trip.

"This is great, I am looking forward to this trip and seeing the family," Sue said with a broad smile.

We piled into the car, and once we got started we told old stories and laughed and soon the driving hours flew by. We both loved having Sue live with us. She liked to eat, never gained a pound, and laughed a lot, chuckled actually. The three of us played cards at night while watching the news. We were all very comfortable together.

Once we arrived and settled in, we made our usual round of visits with Gordon's family and friends in Heart's Delight. We had arrived right at the height of berry picking season, one of my favorite things to do with the kids.

Gordon's niece Mary and her girls brought over their tin cans tied onto strings. We walked behind the house and only a short distance into the woods before we found the low sweet bushes loaded with berries. I looked forward to taking some homemade berry jam back home. I enjoyed the berries with fresh cream too.

Later on that week Gordon and his nephew Gordon, and our neighbors the Crocker's, carried an aluminum canoe deep into the woods to a brook. The water was as clear as glass for catching trout, not really much of a challenge as we could see dozens of them swimming by.

"There were so many we could have scooped them up with a net but that would be cheating," Gordon told them when we got back.

Our trip to Twillingate was such good fun. I was grateful that Sue had come along. We visited Hilda in Twillingate. Sue hadn't seen her in ages, and it was an emotional reunion. Hilda could tell a story with the best of them and joked about the goings on since we left the island. Sue also visited with her husband Frank's family, the Jenkins. None of them were able to attend Frank's funeral, but they all shared their memories and pictures.

Time slipped through our hands, like the slippery trout the men had tried catching. The leaves were turning on the trees, and the air was crisp, a sign for us to return home.

CHAPTER 83

GONE!

1968
GLADYS

We had a long drive back to Boston and I was anxious to get home and see my family. My daughter Dot greeted us. We carried everything from the trunk of the car up the stairs, we sat down in the kitchen, and Dot put the kettle on for tea.

"I have something to tell you," Dot hesitated, and I immediately thought bad news by the tone of her voice.

"Priscilla, Larry, and Kim moved to Florida."

"What? Why would she do that without telling us?" I blurted out.

"Mom, she knew you would be upset but Larry wanted to move where the weather was warmer. His parents are living in Palm Beach Gardens now. I told her you would be heartbroken, especially about Kim leaving."

"What kind of daughter would do that?"

"Gladys, they need their own life. We go to Florida every winter. We'll go to see them." Gordon tried to console me.

"Our kids do what they want. She's an adult now." Sue tried to reason with me, but I was beside myself.

"I just don't understand why she wouldn't call and let us know."

"Ma, I think she thought you would be angry. I was here when they left. They couldn't take the tiger cat and she begged me to take it. You know I can't. Tommy has asthma and he can't have cats," Dot said.

"I'm going to let Angel Memorial pick it up. It will get a good home. She was crying when she left. I'm sure she'll call."

They tried to placate me, but I was inconsolable. I fell into a black depression. How could they leave like that? Gordon told me to let it go. I've never given into depression but this time I couldn't find the energy to get out of bed. Louise, Uldine, and Dot came and coaxed me to see my doctor. They were all pretty mad at Priscilla for being so thoughtless. But most of all, I was heartbroken over losing Kim.

"Hi Mom, it's me Priscilla. I am so sorry but please don't be mad at me." I held the phone but couldn't speak at first. The line stayed silent, then I spoke.

"Why would you leave without telling us?"

"I knew you would be angry and try to talk me out of it. Larry had to go and be there for a new job." She tried to explain it to me.

"My Kim, how is she?"

"She's fine mother, she's okay. Please forgive me," she begged.

"I'm worried about Kim. Where are you living? Is it safe?"

"Right now we're renting in a trailer park in West Palm Beach. Larry is working for a man named Dave. We are going to buy a house soon. You come to Florida every winter and we'll see you then. I'll send you pictures of Kim and our address."

"I love you. Tell Dad I love him too."

The line went dead, she hung up, and I felt my heart breaking.

CHAPTER 84

KIDNEY SURGERY

1969
GLADYS

"Only one of your kidneys is affected, Mrs. Harnum." The doctor proceeded to explain his diagnosis.

"Can I live with only one kidney?" I asked in a panic.

"Of course you can. Your other kidney is fine but the affected one has calcified and that will continue to give you problems and deteriorate. It's best to remove it now."

Gordon sat in the waiting room.

"I want you to explain this to my husband, please."

"Of course, Mrs. Harnum. I'll ask the nurse to bring him in."

After he explained the surgery to Gordon, I asked him about the dangers and recovery. "How will this limit my life?"

"The surgery is reasonably safe as surgeries go. You should be up and about in a few weeks."

"Are you sure the kidney needs to be removed?" Gordon asked.

"Yes. It's not functioning properly and it will, in time, create problems for the good kidney."

The doctor folded his hands and said, "I would never suggest this surgery if I did not deem it absolutely necessary."

"We need to go home and think about all this. We will get back to you this week," I said.

Gordon nodded in agreement and put his hand out to shake the doctor's hand.

"That's fine, just don't leave it too long," he told Gordon.

My daughter Louise did a lot of investigative research that

week into the function of the kidneys and the surgery.

"I think it would be wise to do it, Mom, before other problems develop. You're in pain now and you have too many urinary infections. I promise you, Mom, if you need a kidney after this surgery, I'm glad to donate one of mine."

I started to cry and she did too. "I hope I don't die," I sobbed.

"Where's your faith, Mom? You won't die."

My other daughters decided not to tell Priscilla. She was still living in Florida and would have to fly up with little Kim. No sense worrying her and they agreed they would let her know after the surgery. The surgery was a success, and I only needed a few weeks of recovery. The girls called Priscilla to tell her.

"How could you make a decision not to tell me? What if she died? I would never have been able to tell her how much I loved her. Don't ever keep information like that from me again. I have the right to know!"

She was right of course, but we just wanted to protect her.

CHAPTER 85

LAKEWORTH, FLORIDA

1969
GLADYS

It's been a year since Priscilla and Larry moved to Florida. Gordon and I decided that a month in Florida would get us out of the snow. Of course I looked forward to seeing Priscilla and Kim and Larry.

They were living in a trailer in Jay-Len Trailer Park in Lakeworth. We came to visit and it was a happy reunion. We were both a little reserved with Larry. I felt she had made a wrong choice but I intended to make the best of it. Kim happily paddled along on her Fisher Price scooter. I was overjoyed to see her again.

Larry told us there were deep snake-filled canals on either side of the park. I was even more worried when Priscilla told us that three-year-old Kim had climbed up the bookcase and unhooked the latch on the front door. She was found wandering around the park at 5 a.m. Thank goodness the next-door neighbors were up and invited her in for breakfast. Gordon suggested a drastic measure to scare her into staying home.

"It's horrible," I told him. "We can't do that."

But we did. The neighbors knew the plan. We had Kim tethered around her waist and attached to a tree on a long rope. The neighbors were to walk by and tell her not to run away.

"Sorry Kim, but that's what happens when you run away."

She stretched out her little hands pleading to be released. It was pitiful as we watched out the window. This went on for half an hour until all the neighbors walked by and told her she must not run off again. It worked, but it seemed such a drastic measure.

I never thought we would own a trailer. But the next year we bought a new trailer in a nearby park to stay in for a month in the winter, so I could be closer to Kim and Priscilla.

1970s

CHAPTER 86

DEANNA DOROTHEA

1971
PRISCILLA

Larry and I were just getting by in Florida, and I was pregnant again. I called my mother to tell her.

"Pregnant! That's wonderful news, Priscilla."

But our marriage had been anything but wonderful. Larry's mother actually told me to consider an abortion because she knew Larry was not acting like the decent father and husband he had promised to be. I told her I would never do that. I had asked God for another child and I wanted this baby.

My sisters knew all about his drinking antics, and driving his motorcycle into the living room during my Tupperware party. They also knew about his wild motorcycle friends and his affair.

I considered a divorce, and I told my mother.

"Well, you've made your bed and now you can lie in it, but if you change your mind, you and Kim are welcome to stay here with the new baby."

I knew she'd take us back in a heartbeat. But I was just too proud to give in.

On December 29, 1971 I went into labor. My regular obstetrician had left for another practice. I didn't care for the new doctor that replaced him. Reckless as always, Larry drove so fast to the hospital, and he bounced us so hard over the railroad tracks, I almost had the baby right then and there. He was trying to get to the Bethesda Hospital in Boynton Beach, but the police pulled us over. Realizing the situation, they escorted us to the hospital. The delivery was natural childbirth. That wasn't the plan, but the new doctor was too busy delivering another baby.

Deanna Dorothea arrived with almost no one's assistance, and I was rushed into the delivery room to complete the final process. Uldine flew down a day later to help me with the new baby. When she arrived she found me on the blow up mattress in the bedroom, hemorrhaging.

"I'm calling your doctor and he better do something or you're going to bleed to death."

Larry was so worried by her words he called the doctor.

"Bring her to the hospital right away."

The new doctor had left part of the placenta in, causing me to hemorrhage.

CHAPTER 87

LARRY'S TRAGIC DEATH

1972
PRISCILLA

"I want the baby baptized," Larry said.

"Of course, I planned on doing that."

"Then let's do it soon, Priscilla."

I was surprised that Larry would initiate Deanna's baptism. He was insistent, and it seemed very odd to me. The only church we ever attended was the Good Shepherd Methodist over in West Palm Beach. I called the next day and scheduled the baptism for two weeks. Pam and Charlie, our closest friends in Florida would act as the godparents. They took a picture of Larry holding the baby in her christening gown, with me by his side.

Little did I know at the time, but that would be the last picture of us together. In the mail that week I received a cancellation for our life insurance. That seemed odd too. I distinctly remembered Larry dropping the check off. I went right down to the insurance agency demanding they correct the records and show that it had been paid. They looked in the desk drawer of our agent; he had quit earlier in the month. Sure enough they had our check, un-deposited. Thank goodness they reinstated our life insurance there and then. That whole incident was odd too.

"We need a night out," Larry said to me the following week. "A night out together, just the two of us, no kids."

"That's fine, but I can't ride on the pinion pad yet, Larry, because of my stitches from the baby. Why don't you take the bike? I'll follow you in the Mustang. Let me just call my parents and see if they will babysit."

My parents were down from Boston for the month. They were staying only a few miles away from us. I called them and they said they would be happy to watch Kim and the baby.

The bar in West Palm Beach we were going to was a popular local hang out. On our way there Larry stopped by the self-storage units Larry and his friends used as a clubhouse for the motorcycle club that he belonged to.

"Come on in, Priscilla." I never felt particularly welcome there.

They knew I didn't agree with their lifestyle. Typical motorcycle gang members, they wore black leather and Levi jackets with the sleeves cut off. The back of their jackets were embroidered with the club's gang name. I watched as Larry took off his colors, his Levi vest, and handed them to Ron, one of the club members.

"Now that we have a new baby I think I need to quit the club. Priscilla's sister has an extra lot in New Hampshire and she will give it to us if we want to move back there."

Larry looked at me; we had never discussed moving back before! Of course I wanted to move back, actually in the worst way, but I was shocked to hear him say those words. I decided not to say anything to him after we left. I wasn't really sure that I believed it, any of it. Once again, it seemed odd. He acted unusually thoughtful and kind. Maybe he felt guilty for having an affair while I was pregnant. It was all puzzling me.

We arrived at the locals' bar to a packed crowd; the room was heavy with cigarette smoke. Some people were sitting at the bar and others in the booths. The juke box twanged out a country western song, something about America. We sat down in a booth with a couple that I barely knew.

With a sudden jerk the door to the bar opened and a big muscular guy with tattoos on both arms walked in. He immediately looked over to Larry and started to walk towards our booth. It was apparent to me that he wanted a confrontation. I didn't recognize him but I assumed he was one of the bikers from Larry's club.

Larry leaned over to me and said, "I'm going for a ride on the bike, Priscilla, and I'll be back. I just don't want to get into a fight with that 'FUCK' tonight."

He stood up and headed quickly for the back door. He never returned. I waited and waited until closing time. I was the last person in the bar until the bartender asked me to leave and closed the doors. I stood outside for a while waiting, still no Larry. I walked over to the phone booth outside and called our home number thinking he went home without me. My father answered the phone. What was he doing at my house? I quickly panicked.

"Dad, is Larry there? Is everything alright?" I couldn't keep the panic out of my voice.

"Just come home now dear, I'm waiting for you." I started to tremble uncontrollably. When I arrived home I pulled into the backyard. The police were there with all the lights flashing.

I rushed in and my dad held me. "There's been an accident, Priscilla. Larry is dead."

I cried and shook free. "No! How can you be sure? He can't be dead."

"It's Larry, dear, his boss Dave Wright is going over now to identify the body."

It was Larry. He had been hit head on by a car that pulled into the wrong lane. He died instantly.

CHAPTER 88

RETURNING HOME
WITHOUT LARRY

1972
PRISCILLA

Deanna was born in Boynton Beach in 1971. Two months later Larry had been killed in the tragic motorcycle crash. Almost immediately after the funeral, I knew I wanted to move back home.

MARCH 1972
Uldine called me after the funeral.

"I'll fly down and come get you. We'll all fly back together."

"Oh Uldine, I can't thank you enough. I just can't stay here. I'm getting these sick phone calls just like you warned me. Perverts probably, reading the obituaries and offering sexual favors. I'm afraid to go to sleep. I think someone is at my window or trying to break in. Worse yet I think I'm going to wake out of a deep sleep and see Larry staring at me."

"Try not to worry so much, Priscilla. I'll be down in a few days."

Uldine flew down to accompany me, five-year-old Kim, and my two-month-old baby Deanna. Along for the flight was my Siamese cat with a litter of kittens. Uldine had been down to help me two months earlier, right after Deanna's birth, when I was so ill. We packed only essentials this flight. The rest could be shipped later. I just wanted to get out of Florida and go home.

We boarded the plane to Logan. We were allowed a carrier

with the cat and her kittens under the seat. Just as I looked forward to a quick flight to Boston, the Captain came on the intercom.

"Ladies and gentlemen, due to heavy ice and snow flurries Logan Airport is closed. We will be re-routing your flight to LaGuardia airport in New York. Please check with the gate agent for ground transportation to your final destination."

A moan went through the cabin. We arrived shortly after that and were loaded like sheep onto a bus for the train to Boston. The four of us jammed in one row, plus the cat and her litter of mewling kittens.

We were settling down to a few sandwiches that Uldine had the foresight to make for our trip, when the conductor came by.

He looked into Uldine's kind eyes and asked for her help.

"You look like a kind lady, would you mind keeping a watch over this elderly Italian man in front of you? He does not speak any English and his family will be waiting for him at the station in Boston. He's confused and I don't want him to get off the train until Boston."

"Why yes, of course!" she said.

Every time the train stopped the elderly man got up and looked at Uldine, and she would shake her head "no." He smiled and sat back down. Twenty grueling hours from the time we left Florida we arrived in Boston. Dad and Uldine's second husband, Bill Drown, were there to greet us. It was snowing hard, but what a relief to be home at last.

I rented a tiny place in Acton until I was able to buy some land in Littleton and build a small home. I sold our house in Florida to a woman who had been blinded by a stray bullet. Her friend lived across the street so luckily she bought it right away.

CHAPTER 89

HEBER

1971-1974
GLADYS

Sue and I were sitting at the kitchen table. We were finishing off the last dregs of a pot of coffee. Sue had bought a cheese Danish from the grocer.

"Glad, I think I should move in with Heber. He asked me last month if I would consider it. I'm really going to miss living here with you and Gordon, but Hebe hasn't been well, as you know. He needs someone there to make sure he eats and goes to the doctor and takes his medications correctly."

As sad as I was to see Sue leave, of course she was right. All the years of being a carpenter and breathing in building materials like asbestos had done Heber's lungs in and now he needed our help.

"I'll miss all our good times together, but Heber's place is only a few miles away. You enjoy walking Sue, you can walk to the square in five or ten minutes. Gordon loves the S & S Jewish Deli there. We'll take you and Heber out to lunch after church some Sundays. They make the best pastrami sandwiches in the whole state."

Sue moved in with Heber the next week. The same furnishings were there just as it was when Fannie was alive - the velvet 1950s burgundy overstuffed sofas and chairs, and lamps made of rose plaster, Victorian ladies, and satin shades. The dining room looked almost exactly the same as it was in 1927 for our first dinner there.

I looked out the kitchen window and watched the pigeons land on the flat roof below. The city teemed with life and with all the noises of living very close to your neighbors. I could hear the noise of the tenants next door and below us. The wafting odor of cabbage stuffed with ground beef drifted around the hallway and brought me back twenty years. This apartment was Heber's first investment and it had served him well. What might have been considered slumlord apartments were being converted to condominiums and because Inman Square was close to Boston the values were increasing at a record rate. Who would imagine that the old six-plex would be in such demand?

Poor Heber, even with Sue's ministrations his health continued to decline. His lungs were failing him, black from breathing in asbestos in teardown buildings. He was in and out of the hospital frequently, unable to breathe. We sat with him some times; it was heartbreaking to see him struggling to breathe.

He favored my daughter Louise and made her the executor of his estate. The property was eventually sold and much of the proceeds went to Sue. We were pretty well off and didn't take offense. Sue had only one child, Audrey, and she would leave it all to her someday.

Sadly on a cool autumn day in 1974 Heber drew his last breath and passed away in the hospital. I watched as the yellow and brown leaves swirled around in an eddy at the curb. I wiped the tears from my eyes. Two years later in July of 1976 Sue passed away. Stomach cancer. Although she loved to eat and she stayed thin for years, she smoked a good part of her adult life. I remember her saying that it was okay because she didn't inhale. I never knew if that had anything to do with her cancer, but I always thought it did. I was so lonely without them, but how lucky that they had been in my life. We had laughed a lot, shared our sorrows, and truly loved one another.

Lucy, Heber, Fannie, and Sue are all gone now. It's just my baby sister Hilda back in Twillingate and myself left to share the precious memories of our youth.

CHAPTER 90

STEVEN

1972-1974
LOUISE

We sat on the grassy knoll in my backyard overlooking the small pond. We would iceskate on it in the winter and avoid it in the summer because of the mosquitoes.

Priscilla asked me, "And how is your life, Louise?"

"My life is good."

Priscilla's own life was not so good. She had lost her husband in a tragic motorcycle accident and had two little ones to raise on her own. But I knew our family would all give her their support.

Life had been good to my family. I had a wonderful husband, great kids. We both had good jobs and enough of everything that mattered.

SUMMER'S END 1972

Mom and Dad had just returned from a trip to Newfoundland. They drove up for a Sunday visit.

"Steven looks pale, Louise, I think he's not well."

"Mom, he's fine. He just has no energy. Everyone says it's a growth spurt."

Mom sat at our table with a cup of tea. I could see she wasn't convinced. Dad sat at the table reading the Sunday Globe. He looked over the newspaper at us but didn't comment. Steven came in from helping Fred with yard work.

"Hi Nana and Gramps," he said with a sweet smile.

"Are you feeling okay today, Steven?"

"Sure Nana, why?"

"I just think you're thin and pale."

"I'm always pale and always skinny. I'm fine. Honest."

Later that afternoon after my parents left I looked closer at Steven. Maybe he was too pale. Being so fair skinned and blond made him look pale. I convinced myself he was okay, and Fred didn't think anything was wrong with him either. He shrugged it off as . . . Kids!

Steven started high school that fall, ninth grade, at Acton-Boxborough High. During a morning run at gym class he couldn't keep up with the other boys. The coach yelled at him.

"You can do it, Steve, just keep running strong," he urged Steven on.

"No, I really can't do it. I'm too out of breath."

"You shouldn't be having breathing problems. Ask your mother to take you to the doctor."

Fred and I took Steven to Massachusetts General Hospital for tests. They confirmed a diagnosis Steven had leukemia.

I couldn't imagine anything worse. We learned that leukemia is a cancer that can start in the bone marrow. It leads to the over-production of abnormal white blood cells, the part of the immune system which defends the body against infection. Fred and I were sick with worry. Our beautiful, kind, quiet son had leukemia.

Steven was scheduled for treatment. The chemotherapy and radiation left him weak and sick. He lost his hair from the treatments. He was so young, and he didn't want to die. He fought bravely. We loved him so much and prayed for a remission. The remission came and went. Hope and hopelessness, he died at home on April 27, 1974, only seventeen, but forever in our hearts.

CHAPTER 91

ALL MY GRANDCHILDREN

1973
GLADYS

Our family had grown like wild flowers in a field, random and different in appearance and personality. I had twenty-eight grandchildren in all.

JIM

Jim and Anna had six boys and one girl. Not one looks like the other. Blond haired and blue eyed, or straight hair, curly hair, even frizzy hair. Some with brown eyes, some with hazel.

Jim's temper makes them anxious as if waiting for a reprimand or worse, ducking from a whack. Once, things got so out of control Gordon had to drive to Acton and remove guns from their house. Discipline for Jim's children was sometimes waving the gun. Poor Anna, she was petrified.

Jim didn't like the family meddling but he had gone too far. He gave up the guns for a while, reminding Gordon, "Those are my guns and I want them back, old man."

He called Gordon "old man," never Dad.

ULDINE

Uldine had four girls and two sons; she's the calmest of my children. She is quiet and patient, but most of all, loving. Two girls looked like her and two favor Howie. Earl and Brian favor the Harnums. Four years after Howie died, Uldine married Bill Drown. He loved her and her children. His ability to listen and reason gained the love and respect of all her children.

211

LOUISE

Louise and Fred had three boys and a girl. Elizabeth and David looked like Louise, while poor Steven had been a carbon copy of Fred; Rick was a mixture of both. They are all practical and frugal. The children were taught that education is very important and to "waste not, want not." They love their children but expect them to participate in responsibility. They live in the country with a nice garden, chickens, and a mulch pile. They pick blueberries and apples and everyone can cook.

GORDON

Gordon and Pearl have two sons Kirby and Doug. Handsome boys. They had a good life with a nice home and a pool. They had enough money to be extravagant; too bad they are divorced now. Young Gordon always had a roving eye; he was too charming, too smart, and had too much money. He and his new wife Donna have a son Keith. They are pretty well suited, or at least it seems so.

DOT

Dot and Tom have a son Tommy and a daughter Debbie. They've done quite well for themselves. Tom's still at the post office and does well with stock market tips from rich residents in the town where he works. Dot is also working as a hostess. They invested wisely in the stock market and own a lovely home. Tom is home early from his route and stays with the kids while Dot goes to work. We call Dot "Dutch Cleanser." She's always scrubbing and cleaning. Dot is full of energy whereas Tom seems calm, lethargic even. They get along well together.

BILL

Bill and Frannie have four children: Linda, Billy, Philip, and Jill. Linda is quite pragmatic and already has direction. Billy and

Philip are loveable but look out, those innocent countenances set the house on fire one time! They love playing cowboys and Indians in the middle of the night, waking everyone up. Jill is the baby in the family, and like most babies she's given a little more attention. Bill has filled a position in the business that suits him. He is on the road a lot, estimating jobs. He was never one to sit at a desk.

PRISCILLA

Priscilla moved back home since Larry's death. She is too young to be widowed. No father for her children. Kim takes after her in looks, but Priscilla is hard on her. She expects her to behave all the time. Deanna is still a baby. I told Priscilla she loves Deanna more than Kim; she was mad at me for saying that. Sometimes I wish I would bite my tongue. She has found a piece of land and it's only one mile from Louise and Fred. She is building a home and barn there. Finally she will get her horse.

CHAPTER 92

MINK JACKET

1977
GLADYS

"In all the fifty years we've been married, Gladys, I haven't given you as many gifts for Christmas and birthdays as I wanted. I give you a card with money sometimes, but I'm not good at choosing nice gifts. I know you have always wanted a fur coat, so I would like to get you one to celebrate our 50th anniversary."

"Oh Gordon! You know I've always wanted a mink jacket. I appreciate the offer but honey they're expensive, thousands of dollars."

I was so pleased that he offered, and truly I wanted a mink.

"Glad, remember the fur I got you on that first trip back to Newfoundland? I bought you the full Lynx pelt. I wrapped it around my belly for you and then I hid it under my coat so I wouldn't be stopped at the border.

I smiled, "Yes, I remember that. I kept it rolled up and wrapped in a bag in the cedar closet. It's still there. It horrified the grandkids when I pulled it out, with its beady eyes and sharp fangs. I don't know what you thought I was supposed to do with it, but I guess it's the thought that counts."

I had kept that pelt in the cedar closet for all these years because I didn't want to hurt Gordon's feelings.

"So, now I'm going to make it up to you. Make an appointment at the furriers in Boston and you can pick out whatever you want. Okay, Glad?"

"Thank you so much, Gordon. I've wanted a mink jacket for years. I'll call Kakas Furriers and make an appointment."

Kakas Furriers were renowned for the finest fur coats in Boston and here we were to pick one out for me. I was so excited. The salesperson picked out a gorgeous mink jacket with wide cuffs, and sized for a petite person. He slipped it on me and it felt custom made for me. I'm sure I blushed as I looked into the long mirrors. I looked elegant. No longer the skinny plain girl from Twillingate.

Gordon had a broad smile. "It's yours."

The salesman said it would be ready for pick-up in a few days. My initials - GCH in large sweeping letters - were embroidered into the silk lining. Gordon happily wrote the check.

CHAPTER 93

50th

WEDDING ANNIVERSARY

1977-1978
GLADYS

1977 would see my 50th year of marriage to Gordon. I was in the mood to celebrate and of course I wanted my family gathered around me.

"Fifty years, it should be a celebration. Don't you think, Gordon?"

"Yes, Gladys, we've seen a lot in those years and damn, . . ." I jumped as he slapped his hand on the kitchen table, ". . . a celebration is in order!"

"Maybe Fantasia's in Fresh Pond?"

"Great, let's make arrangements. Anything you want."

"It's a good reason to get family together. I'll get right on it. I'd love a celebration." I smiled at the thought of a great party.

The girls helped with all the arrangements, invitations, flowers, and menu. I wanted to look my best, so I went to the gown shop in Watertown and found the perfect gown. Simple beige beaded around the bodice and draped to floor length.

"We also need a photographer, Ma," Louise said and she took on the job of finding one.

For the menu I chose roast beef, mashed potatoes, asparagus, gravy and rolls, and a nice dessert. Frannie offered to make the cake. She makes beautiful cakes.

"The invitation will be simple," I told Gordon, "and no gifts, right?"

"No gifts, we don't need a thing. How blessed are we not to need anything!"

I went over the guest list one last time. We invited all the children, grandchildren, and our two great-grandchildren. We also invited our friends from church, our old friends from Newfoundland, and some of our neighbors. We invited Fred's sister Jennie and Uncle Bill's family. I didn't want to slight anyone.

Gordon put on his brown suit and bow tie. After all these years, he still looked handsome to me. My hair was mostly grey, but Gordon had all his hair with only a touch of grey at the temples. God had been so good to us. We've lived these fifty years together through good, bad, and sad.

"We are luckier than most, Glad." He hugged me.

I hugged him back, I didn't want to cry and ruin my makeup. Dot had applied it so carefully moments before.

I walked through the door with Gordon, resplendent in my new mink jacket.

There were over one hundred family and guests including the minister who said grace. The photographer took a wonderful picture of the two of us and went from table to table getting candid shots. He lined up all our family for a group photo, one we would cherish forever.

Photo on page 215
Gladys and Gordon Harnum at their 50th Wedding Anniversary party in 1977

1980s

CHAPTER 94

DANNY & GARY

1979-82
PRISCILLA

Things were always up in the air with my brother Jim and his sons, so I wasn't too surprised when I got a phone call from my nephews Neal and Paul, his eldest boys. I called my mom to discuss the situation.

"Mom, Jim's son Paul called. He wants me to get guardianship for Danny and Gary. Now that Ann and Jim are divorced they've basically abandoned the boys. Jim put the house on the market, and no one told the boys. They came home one day to find a 'For Sale' sign in the yard and the house completely empty."

"Neal and Paul took Danny and Gary to Florida with them. They were out of money, and Neal and Paul were caught shoplifting. Danny and Gary had not committed any crime, however because they're minors they've been sent to a juvenile detention center. Paul says they need a responsible relative to take guardianship."

"They're going to need a place to live, dear God, let me talk to your father about this. What a mess! Priscilla, are you sure you're willing to take them in? They're teenagers, it's going to be a lot of responsibility and expense."

I didn't hesitate, "Of course I am, Mom."

"Your father and I will help you with food and electricity, and whatever else they might need."

Dad agreed to the plan, so I filed for custody. I was grateful they offered to help. I would be faced with an enormous responsibility, but there was no way I was going to leave those boys to fend for themselves or worse, be put in the state foster system. But I needed my brother's permission for custody. Actually getting custody turned out easier than I thought. My brother Jim called me and he was only too happy to give them up, and he agreed to let me have custody.

"I hope they give you as much shit as they gave me," he said.

"They'll be just fine." I wondered what kind of crap comment that was. Ann never responded one way or the other, and I guess she didn't need to respond. I didn't have a clue of her whereabouts anyway. It was overwhelming, but I was in it for the long haul now.

I was widowed and Kim was running loose around Littleton, which kept me awake at nights with worry or driving around looking for her. Deanna was probably doing things that I didn't know about, but she kept quiet about it.

The boys moved in and they were angry. I couldn't blame them; they didn't deserve to be thrown out of their own home. They had done nothing wrong and they deserved a break. I didn't know how qualified I was going to be at parenting them, but I was going to try my best. Their aunt Louise and uncle Fred lived a mile away and I knew they would be supportive.

My other brother Bill, the boys' uncle, lived in the next town. He had four kids of his own to deal with, but I knew he would be supportive. Likewise their uncle Gordon was only a call away. But it wasn't all that easy in the end.

I had to go to the Littleton High School and plead with the principal on their behalf. I wanted them in the correct grade level for their age. It did not follow the school rules but they agreed. I also wanted Gary to be on the football team. This also was not a normal procedure at Littleton, but they agreed. I felt the boys needed to get back to normalcy and a routine lifestyle.

The boys didn't look a bit like brothers in appearance or

personality. Danny was tall, slim, and fair with blue eyes and curly blond hair. Gary was short with a stocky build like a football halfback. He had dark brown hair and eyes. Gary's opinion of the world was "Don't mess with me!" and "I'm going to be successful in spite of everything and everyone."

Danny suffered with anxiety and claustrophobia; he avoided conflict because his confidence had been beaten down. It was small wonder that the boys didn't have much trust.

Living together was an adjustment for all of us. Sometimes it was a crazy house. On a few occasions when I went away for the weekend my house became party central. Once my brother Bill had to go to my house and break up their party after the police were called. It was all part of having a house full of teenagers.

Danny graduated that following year from high school and Gary a year later. My parents helped Gary with four years of college and Danny started at Middlesex. They survived a very dysfunctional youth, but they did well and I was proud of them. Today they continue to be happy and successful.

CHAPTER 95

ARIZONA OR BUST!

1982 -1983
PRISCILLA

I had been avoiding the phone for a while; my mother had been calling me constantly. I picked up the handle and dialed my parents' number.

"Hi Priscilla, I'm so glad you finally called me back."

"Yes, Mum, you're going to be upset when I tell you this, but please, hear me out."

"Priscilla, what's wrong?" I could hear the edge in her voice.

"Mum, Kim is involved with a kid who peddles drugs at her high school. She's run off and I'm driving around every night trying to find her. She always did so well in school and now that has changed too. Mum, what do you think? I'm going to take Kim and Deanna to Scottsdale, Arizona for the year. It will take her away from that kid. He and his friends are taking her down a dark path and I'm afraid of what might happen."

"But why Arizona? It's so far away. What about your house and the horse? It sounds too drastic. Who do you know there? What about a job? Why don't you stay here or go to New Hampshire, that's not so far away." I knew she would try to persuade me out of this drastic measure, but I held firm.

"Fran and Bill have friends in Arizona, Linda and Sam Vidulich, they will watch out for us. They're good Christian people and they live in Scottsdale. It's a good time to do it. Jim's boys are finally out of my house and on their own now. I've helped them as much as I can. They're both in college. I've been there for them when they needed me and now I need to concentrate and reconnect with Kim."

"I can rent my house out and that will give me some income until I get a job. I'm hoping a change of schools and some new friends should get her back on track." I remembered how hard it was for me when Mum decided I should change schools and attend Belmont High.

"I've already found a house there to rent. Linda Daisy, my neighbor has agreed to take care of my horse, Jericho.

"Priscilla, I don't feel good about this, but you are just like your father, strong willed and you won't listen to anyone."

My sister Louise had promised to drive to Arizona with us. I was grateful to her for that. God bless her, she's a good sister. Ironically, G.H. Harnum had an empty truck and trailer heading out west. They took all my furniture and even the piano to Scottsdale.

The house was rented to some employees from New Balance Shoes. My horse Jericho went to Linda Daisy's and was in good care. Kim and Deanna were not thrilled at all, but they were willing to go on an adventure. The tan Honda Accord was loaded with our ancient Siamese cat, Tasha. After a little mewling she settled in on the wide dashboard and off we drove to Arizona with Louise in shotgun. As we drove through the desert, a magnificent rainbow crossed over us from one side of the road to the other. We considered it a good sign.

Louise called me. "Let me call you right back. It's Mum calling again." My mother had been calling constantly and shortly after I hung up with Louise, Mom called back.

"Priscilla, I'll feel better when you and the girls move back from Arizona. Every time I call and ask to speak to Kim, she's not there. I'm worried, I think something strange is going on."

I heard my dad talking to her in the background.

"Gladys, I'm sure things are fine. Priscilla would tell you if she had a problem. You worry too much."

My father's words somehow were not comforting to her. I

could hear her put her hand over the receiver, but I could still hear their conversation.

"I haven't spoken to Kim since they moved and we've always been so close. I won't deny it, she is my favorite granddaughter."

"You spoiled her, Gladys. You covered her lies and made excuses when she stole things. She even broke into our house here. Made it look like a burglary. Took the roast beef we had for supper. I hope she smartens up out there," my dad sounded disgusted. "I know she didn't have a father, but I didn't either. No excuses." I quickly said goodbye and hung up the phone.

PRISCILLA RETURNS
GLADYS

In a way I felt glad I didn't know what happened to Priscilla in Arizona. She and the girls had driven to Scottsdale, Arizona with Louise and the old Siamese cat.

Priscilla drove the whole way, like her father she enjoyed driving. The home they rented was in a neighborhood of similar slab ranches and friendly neighbors. Her furniture arrived the same day they did. Louise helped her settle in and then flew back home.

Now Priscilla was back from Arizona, and we sat at my kitchen table while she let the story unfold.

"Getting a job was my first priority. I applied everywhere without much luck. Kim looked for a job too. She applied at Arby's and got a job in the kitchen."

Priscilla continued, "We attended the Scottsdale Bible Church and through the church network, I got a job at an insurance marketing company. I hated the job, Ma, but I needed it."

"I enrolled Kim and Deanna in school, and we spent weekends tubing down the Colorado River and day tripping

223

over the Mexican border to shop. The Grand Canyon was about three hours away. We enjoyed it so much, we went seven times, and we also went to the carnival in Phoenix."

I knew there was another story in all this, and I wondered when she'd get to it.

"About a month later, I came home from work one day and Kim was gone. There was a group of men putting cable TV lines in the front of our rental. I ran out and asked them if they had seen my daughter, a pretty blond girl, leave the house."

"Yah," they volunteered, "looked like she had her stuff loaded in a bag. She was carrying a small TV into a van with a bunch of kids."

"My heart sank, Mom. I filed a missing persons report with the police. I made up posters and taped them at the Paradise Mall and throughout our neighborhood. The neighborhood even held a prayer vigil for us."

"Oh, Priscilla! Why didn't you call us?"

"I just couldn't, Mom. I felt so terrible, but that's why she was never here when you called. I was too embarrassed to tell you. If she never came back you would never forgive me. Four months later she called me, and I can remember her words exactly - 'Hi Ma, it's Kim. Are you mad at me?'"

"I couldn't believe it, she had joined a carnival of all things, and went off to California. I thought taking her far away from the trouble in Littleton would solve her problem. But I learned the hard way you can't run away from your problems, you just take them with you."

"I could have told you that, Priscilla, and I'm sure I did over the years. Sometimes you just have to learn at your own school of hard knocks."

"We're back for good now, Mom. I'm so grateful."

I was upset naturally, but I bit my tongue. I didn't want to say anything more disparaging to her.

"Priscilla, I knew something wasn't right. I told your father that. I kept you in my prayers. I suppose I should have realized that making excuses for Kim's behavior made things worse. But I do love her so much. Well, what will you do about school?"

"I've enrolled her at Newman Prep. I can only hope she will get back on the right path."

CHAPTER 96

LAST TRIP
TO NEWFOUNDLAND

1983
GLADYS

It was 1983 and my husband Gordon's health had been up and down. Never deterred by any obstacle, Gordon decided we should go on one last trip to Newfoundland. We would stop at St. John's, Heart's Delight, and my hometown Twillingate. I should have been over the moon, but I wasn't. He wanted his brother Bill to come along with us.

Bill is in worse health than Gordon, I thought out loud.

Luckily no one heard me, and over my objection, he got his way and called his brother Bill.

"Bill, Gladys and I are going to Newfoundland. I don't know about you, but it may be my last trip. Do you want to come with us?"

"Yes boy," he used the vernacular title "boy." "I would. I been feeling poorly lately, but I'd like to make one last trip home."

"Yup, same here with me, Bill. Those kidney stones have done a number on me," Gordon sadly replied.

"Gordon, I don't think you're well enough to drive all that way. Your brother Bill isn't in much better shape than you," I told him.

"I'll be fine. I want to go."

"Well, I can't drive, Gordon, and I don't think your brother Bill will be much help."

"Glad, I want to go. I'll pack light then. We won't be there but a few weeks."

We took our time going through Nova Scotia to the ferry. I

felt nervous as a cat. Gordon was driving. He drove much slower than usual and he looked pale. Bill sat in the back seat and complained of stomach pain. What would I do if they couldn't drive? We would be stranded in the middle of nowhere. It was the one time in my life I really regretted not learning to drive. Thank God, we finally made it to the ferry with no incident and Gordon drove the car on.

We had our own cabin. It was a tight fit but there were bunks. Both men lay down and dozed off before the ferry left port. I sat on the bunk wanting to sleep. I finally gave in and slept a short time. Gordon woke me up with his coughing.

"I'm feeling sick, Glad."

He wasn't seasick and he kept everything down. I handed him two aspirins and a cup of water from the tiny sink.

I nagged, "We never should have come. You're a stubborn man, Gordon."

We reached shore several hours later, a new day's sun just rising up over the horizon. Maybe things will get better now, I hoped. I was grateful the ocean had been calm and looked out over the view as we chugged our way into berth.

"We made it!" Gordon said as we pulled into the driveway.

Trinity Bay glistened, a deep dark blue, as pale icebergs floated by past the harbor, snowy aqua peaks drifting with the current. It took my breath away, what a beautiful sight.

Once we were out of the car, I took hold of the reins again.

"Leave the bags," I told them. "We can get them later. Take the groceries in, let's sit down and have a cup of tea." I encouraged them as they slowly climbed one step at a time into the house. It was an agonizing effort for both of them.

Our Newfie relatives had turned on the electricity before we arrived; I turned the heat up a bit and unloaded the groceries.

Bless them! They had left a cake, tin milk, a loaf of homemade bread, and a jar of partridgeberry jam in the fridge.

Both Gordon and Bill looked beat as they ate the small lunch I put together. They were both chilled to the bone being unaccustomed to the cooler weather. They went to the bedrooms and took a nap. I called young Gordon at home as they slept. I needed someone to listen.

"Son, they are both too sick to be here, but it's important that they are here and I understand that. I just can't stop from worrying about them. What if something happens to them, Gordon?"

"Maybe they will both be better tomorrow," he said, trying to encourage me.

Thank goodness, the following day they were better. We drove around the bay at Heart's Delight to visit Eva and Ambrose's children and grandchildren. Eva and Ambrose had passed on and so had Gordon and Bill's half-sister, Priscilla, but there were still plenty of relatives for us to visit.

Our nephew Gordon and his wife were still in the same house that Gordon and Bill were born in. Most likely they would stay there the rest of their lives. Of their ten children only one stayed in Heart's Delight.

The rest were grown and gone, on to Labrador or St. John's, or off the island altogether. Verna their oldest still lived in Heart's Delight with her husband Al. They were just a stone's throw away from the family home. It was so nice to be greeted with open arms and Gordon lit up instantly. I watched, relieved as the color came back to his face.

Bill, usually quiet and unemotional, showed signs of joy. Then I realized just how important it was for them to take this journey. A cold shiver went up my spine, and it wasn't from the icy Newfoundland weather. I feared it would be Gordon and Bill's last journey.

Mary fussed around the wood stove preparing our meal. They still used it for cooking and warmth.

"The tea will be ready in just a bit. Sit down and take a load off . . . please sit down. It does my heart good to see all of you." Mary gave us a broad smile.

There were a few changes in the kitchen but most notable was the loss of Eva and Ambrose - they were so much a part of that picture. Mary was happy, but older looking. She was still the long-suffering wife, mother, chief cook, and bottle washer. Her red hair streaked grey from the years but her smile was as warm and generous as ever.

Nephew Gordon had gotten heavier; he looked a bulk of a man. He parked himself at the head of the long hand-hewn table and ordered Mary to lay food and cake on the table.

"You must be famished!" He invited us to dig in.

Mary served fresh biscuits with churned butter and a piping hot fish stew.

"No, just a long trip. Not as young as we used to be," Gordon added.

"We have a big garden this year, we've done well. We go around in the truck, the old Ford out back. Mary takes the vegetables door to door."

I could see that scene easily. Gordon sitting on his arse in the truck while Mary climbed up and down the hills to every house peddling vegetables. Oh, nothing against him, he's always been polite to me. But I thought back to the time Gordon paid for his nephew's ticket to the States for a visit. He sat at our dinner table. "I'll try some of them thar' peaches, Aunt Gladys." They were actually apricots and I had to suppress a laugh.

I wanted to take a drive to St. John's to see Bill and Marion, Jen and Lena Minnie. Thankfully the roads were paved now and I was hoping for an easy drive.

"Uncle Gordon, I kin drive ya there."

"I think I'm fine. It's only an hour." Bill wanted to say hello too, so off we went.

Our visit in St. John's was just a daytrip. They set a table for us, a meat platter with cheese and cake and tea. A local meat platter is actually sandwich meat with bread in a basket if you want to make a regular sandwich. The lunch was accompanied with homemade pickles, mustard, or mayonnaise. We washed it all down with lots of tea, steeped in an old-fashioned china teapot.

Gordon's nephew Bill Wiltshire worked on the train. He's a pleasant man. Marion is a small frail lady, quiet and very kind. Also there is Jen. We love Jen, although she does go on about every cold or ailment. They keep her close to home for fear of germs. Lena's a real character, with a no nonsense attitude, wearing dated brown oxfords and always in her Salvation Army uniform. She can't stay at home, and has to go out. She can't be bothered with all this talk of sickness, and I secretly agreed with her. After hugs and a wink she's off to save the world.

We traveled back that evening with Gordon doing a passable job at driving. We drove by quaint villages and beached fishing dories along the coast as the evening settled into dusk.

After a day of rest I looked forward to an overnight with my sister Hilda and Pete in Twillingate.

"Gordon, it's a four hour drive. If you're not up to it, I'll get someone to drive us there."

"No, Glad, I can make it."

We drove along at a snail's pace. Bill snoozed in the back seat. In the distance I saw a bridge across to the island of Twillingate. That's new! The smell of the sea was strong and filled my lungs. Hilda and Pete's house stands tall, across from the beach where we grew up.

Hilda's son Jack owns the home I was born and grew up in. It has been modernized and doesn't look anything like the original. We pulled up and Hilda came out to greet us. Her hair completely grey now, like mine, and parted in the middle, it's cropped short but thick like a wedge on either side of the part. Her face is flat and reminds me of Mother and her possible Beothuk heritage.

"Come in, come in, Glad. Gordon, do you need a hand?"

His legs were shaky after the long drive, and he is noticeably bent over. Bill is not much better. There is only Hilda and me left now. Lucy and Sue and Heber have all gone before us.

The path on the side of the house had eight painted black headstones. No bigger than a small book with the names of all her dogs that passed on. She calls them "crackies" not dogs. Most of them were mixed breed. Maybe Spitz. To the right is the garden, memories flood back to me. It is still well tended. This is where my parent's toiled, tilling and planting.

"Find a seat at the table!" Pete invited us. Another luncheon and more food set on the table. Jam and bread with a steaming pot of tea.

"I've got a fish and brewis for you, just like Mother used to make."

I said, "It looks delicious, Hilda. You shouldn't have gone to so much trouble."

"Of course I had to, you're my big sister." I am all choked up with emotion; I move over to the big stove and rub my hands. There is a pot of fish on the burner and the scent fills the room.

"Jack caught them fresh this morning. He and Florence will be over in a bit. He is mad at the Canadians again. They've restricted our fishing areas and have given rights to the Japanese and the Russians. He's so mad he hung the Canadian flag upside down in protest. Some good that will do." Hilda laughed and Gordon laughed with her.

CHAPTER 97

THE RIDE HOME

1983
GLADYS

We were getting ready for the long journey home and I could see Gordon was doing poorly and Bill was faring no better. I called young Gordon in a panic.

"Your father and Uncle Bill are in pretty bad shape. They will never be able to drive home; he wants you and Dot to fly up here. Dot can drive them home and I'll fly back with you."

I never even considered flying back on my own and it was important for young Gordon to return to the business without delay.

"Sure, Ma. I'll call Dot and get flights out. Don't worry, Ma. I'll get you all home safe and sound. I'll call you back right away." Bless him, I thought.

"It's going to be fine. They'll fly up and get us," I told Bill and Gordon.

Even with his hearing aid out, Gordon heard the phone ringing.

"Get the phone, Gladys!"

"Take it easy, I'm getting it."

"Hi, Ma, it's Dot."

"Oh Dot, they're both so sick, too weak to drive," I said lowering my voice.

"Don't worry, Ma. I'll fly down and drive them back. This is going to be the trip from Hell, I can tell you right now. You notice how Dad always calls me when he needs something? Me, who's afraid to drive, with two sick old men."

"Please, Dot. Don't start in now, he's depending on you." I

tried to placate her with little success.

"Oh well, you know I'll do it."

"Your brother Gordon can't do the drive, he has to run the business."

"I know the business is more important than me. Besides, if Dad and Uncle Bill are sick on the side of the road, Gordon would be out there puking his guts out with them. Ha-ha!"

We closed up the house, and said our goodbyes. I was so relieved to be heading home.

CHAPTER 98

DOT DRIVES BACK

1983
DOT

We met Mom and Dad at the airport and traded off. I was shocked at how poorly Dad and Uncle Bill looked. My mother and brother returned to the terminal and I took over the driving. I could see how relieved Dad was, but now I was the one that had to deal with them. Uncle Bill was in the back seat and looked a little green around the gills. We managed to get to the ferry in one piece.

"Now Dad, there's only one thing. I don't think I can drive this car onto the ferry."

"Move over, Dot! I'll drive it in. You're too close to the other cars, Dot."

He waved me away. When we arrived at port on the other end, Dad was so exhausted he couldn't drive the car off.

"You can do it, Dot. Just drive the car!" It was at this point I realized the seriousness of my father's health. Dad had never been afraid to take a chance or try something new. He had climbed skyscrapers, scaled towers, driven giant trucks, and operated heavy equipment. Now, here I was, driving him on what should have been a rather long but pleasant journey.

My nerves were frayed. Uncle Bill sat silent in the back seat, looking sicker by the mile. I thought, please don't die back there. What the hell would I do then? Every so many miles I had to stop for them to pee on the side of the road or throw their guts up. Then matters turned worse, we had a flat tire on a double highway. I never changed a tire in my life!

Unbelievably despite their current situation, Dad and Uncle Bill, too weak to really help, managed to dart traffic to get some boards laying on the other side of the road. They could barely walk, let alone run.

"Dad!" I shouted. "You're crazy! You're gonna get hit by a car!"

They didn't, and they brought back a couple of boards to raise the tire high enough to jack it up. Fat chance! They couldn't do it.

Angels must have taken pity on us because a trucker pulled over to help.

"It's my father and uncle. They're both very sick."

"I got this, sir. Let me do this for you."

Dad thanked him and moved out of the way. He fixed the wheel, waved, and drove off down the highway.

We arrived in Boston and dropped Uncle Bill off in Somerville on the way. I told him to get to the doctor, then drove Dad another fifteen minutes to Belmont.

We got Dad to a doctor that week. It wasn't good news. He told us Dad's kidneys were failing. Two years later he started dialysis.

He'd passed kidney stones a good part of his life and it was painful but dialysis was a death warrant to him.

CHAPTER 99

DOT MOVES TO FLORIDA

1983
DOT

I had just recovered from my nightmare drive through Newfoundland with Dad and Uncle Bill, when Tom and I decided it was time to visit my parents and let them know the big news. Tom and I were moving to Florida! We stopped by Mom's on a Saturday with the kids to say goodbye.

"You'll be so far away, Dot." I could hear the upset in my mother's voice.

'Ma, I can fly up anytime," I consoled her, even though I hated to fly.

"Tom has already had a heart attack and a by-pass. The post office has given him disability retirement."

"I'm fifty-three," Tom told Ma. "I could have another heart attack any time."

"I understand, you need to move to warmer weather and retire. I'm sure you deserve it," Ma said.

"You do what you have to do," Dad chimed in.

I tried to comfort Ma. "Louise and Fred are only a half hour away from you and Priscilla is back from Arizona now, she's only a mile from there."

My sister Uldine had moved to New Hampshire, and she was two hours away. My brother Bill lived in Westford not too far a drive. Gordon lived in New Hampshire. He had remarried a lady named Donna and he stopped by our parents' house all the time. Jim moved to New Hampshire and remarried but remained distant. There was plenty of family for Ma, I thought, but I explained all that to Ma, again.

"It's okay, Dot. I understand. I need to be grateful everyone is so close."

"It's the perfect time, Ma. Debbie is fourteen, she'll start high school in Florida when we move. Tommy's at Boston University, he's going to stay up here too."

"I want to be a cardiologist," Tommy proudly announced to his grandparents. Tom had been grooming our son to study cardiology because of his family's history of heart disease.

"We bought a nice condo last week. It's facing the ocean. Only one small problem - my claustrophobia. I can't get in the elevator, so I'll get my exercise walking up and down five flights of stairs to walk the dogs. I've figured out the groceries too. I just put the bags in the elevator on the first floor, push the button to the fifth floor, and run like hell up the five flights to meet it!"

We all had a good laugh, at my own expense!

236

CHAPTER 100

UNCLE BILL HARNUM

1984
GLADYS

Gordon had been admitted to Mount Auburn Hospital and was recovering from pneumonia. He contracted a staph infection in the hospital and that delayed his healing for another two weeks. Brother Bill stopped by one afternoon to see him.

"Hiya Gordon, I just stopped by to see how you're coming along."

"Not so good, Bill, not so good." Gordon mustered a weak smile.

I noticed Bill looked quite frail himself, and his color wasn't all that good.

"I've not been so good myself," he remarked, jerking me out of my assessment.

We sat in the hospital room, a dark gloomy day outside, all gathered around Dad's bed. Priscilla, Louise, and Fred were with me. We hovered around Uncle Bill making sure he was comfortable. We didn't see him that often, but it seemed to me that he had grown friendlier and kinder over the years. Now I wished we had encouraged more interaction between our two families.

In 1972 when Priscilla's husband died in the motorcycle crash, Bill had flown down to Florida with Dot. He and Dot both had a fear of flying. But she said they would be fine if they flew together.

"Uncle Bill, I just want to thank you again for flying down when Larry died," Priscilla said.

"You can thank Dot for that. She can be very convincing when she makes her mind up and she can really make you laugh." We all laughed at that. Even Gordon.

Poor Uncle Bill, he died before Gordon left the hospital. We didn't say anything to Gordon thinking he might have a relapse.

Gordon stayed in the hospital another few weeks and maybe it was wrong of us not to tell him, after all Bill was his only brother. The doctors said Bill had stomach cancer. He knew all along, but never told anyone.

CHAPTER 101

GORDON HEDLEY HARNUM

1987
GLADYS

After two years of kidney dialysis Gordon's veins were collapsing. The doctors said he couldn't remain on dialysis without going into kidney failure. The next day the hospital called back and said they could try one other alternative method. Gordon was hopeful and he agreed to try it, and so we were all hopeful after that.

Priscilla had been by the house the day before to see him. She had written a letter to Gordon to thank him for all the help he had given her over the years. He was resting quietly in bed but sat up to read it when she arrived.

On the quiet, she told me she had to write the letter because she was afraid she would just cry if she had to read it out loud. Gordon read through it and looked at her and said, "Thank you. I love all my girls."

Gordon never was one to say "I love you." It just wasn't in him, but he showed his love, to all of us, in many other ways. Priscilla watched him read the letter and she cried anyway. The next morning Gordon got dressed, ready for his ride to the hospital. He felt quite hopeful about the new treatment.

I was busy stirring his cream of wheat on the stove. He had just finished a cup of coffee and toast. I jumped back when I heard the crash. He had banged his head on the kitchen table.

"Gordon, Gordon! Come back," I cried to him.

Rita came running into the kitchen. She had been helping us with his care for the last month.

"What's wrong?"

"Call 911! I think he's dead." Rita didn't hesitate. She called, and the paramedics arrived minutes later. The hospital was only a mile away. They worked on Gordon, pumping his chest in the ambulance but it was all to no avail.

"Ma'am, we are not getting any response. We are so very sorry."

They drove him straight to Sancta Maria Hospital around the corner. Rita called the boys and my daughters.

"Oh, God," I sobbed out loud. "What will I do without you?"

What would I do?

Gordon and Bill drove straight to the hospital. They came back to the house and told me when they walked in to identify their father they almost believed he was still alive. His eyes were still wide open, the same brilliant blue as ever.

CHAPTER 102

FAREWELL TO GORDON

1987
GLADYS

Long's Funeral Home was next to St. James's Church on Massachusetts Avenue in Cambridge. Our family and friends had relied on the owners, Dick Long especially, to preserve the dignity of our loved ones that had passed. They had personally met almost every person that they had provided a wake and burial for.

My girls went with me to pick out the casket. It was not ornate but solid like my husband with no fancy decoration, just like him. Gordon looked handsome in his navy suit and blue favorite necktie. His hair had a hint of grey at the temples. God I'll miss him, I'll miss those strong hands and his laughter. I'll miss him coming up the stairs from the garage with a bag of pastry for dessert. He had such a sweet tooth.

It was almost unbearable to look at him in the casket. Gone from me, but not forever, I knew he was in Heaven, and I would see him again, but for now that was little consolation. My faith was wavering. I wanted him to be here on Earth.

There were so many flowers they filled the stairways and halls. Gordon was never one for flowers, but he had enough for his entire lifetime lining the funeral parlor. Hundreds of family, friends, employees, and business associates poured through the doors to pay their respects and say their goodbyes.

So many tears were shed. Each one passing me with condolences saying how much he was loved and respected. He was an honest businessman, a deacon of the church, a Mason, and always very generous.

As the hearse left for Puritan Lawn Cemetery and Memorial Park in Peabody cars lined up along Massachusetts Avenue for as far as the eye could see. They followed us onto Route 128. You could see their lights for miles behind us, such a tribute. I hoped he was looking down and seeing how much he meant to so many people. I thought of those words again: He gave more than he took back. I believed the world was a little better because of him.

ENTER ANNA
1987
GLADYS

After Gordon died it became apparent that I needed someone to stay with me. I wasn't afraid to be alone but I had a car and I didn't drive, I never did get a driver's license, and so I became very dependent on other people taking me about.

I was still very much involved in church and the church thrift shop. There was the Eastern Star at the lodge and I liked to shop and entertain and of course I always enjoyed playing Bingo and visiting with my family.

Jim's ex-wife Anna returned to the area and we contacted her. She didn't have any family locally besides us and she needed a place to stay and a small income. Anna could drive, so it was an obvious choice for both of us and she moved in with me.

CHAPTER 103

ST. JAMES'S CHURCH, CAMBRIDGE

November 1988
PRISCILLA

The collection of old stained glass church windows facing Massachusetts Avenue were in a sad state of disrepair.

My sisters and I thought that replacing the old windows with a larger than life nativity scene dedicated to our father's memory would be an appropriate gift to the church. Louise did some research and connected with Lyn Hovey, a renowned stained glass artist. We all agreed to hire him for the task.

On the day of the dedication the church was filled. My mother had asked if I would do the dedication speech. I was prepared and I just hoped I wouldn't cry, at least not too much.

"Today is a very special day for our family. We are happy that so many of you came out to share it with us. My father Gordon Harnum died just over a year ago. He was an extraordinary man and we all miss him. He believed that honesty and hard work paved the road to success. He believed in God and he believed in himself."

"With little more than a pocketful of dreams, he left Newfoundland and set forth for America. On his journey he met Gladys Primmer, the future Mrs. Gordon Harnum, and our mother. They married soon after, right here at St. James's Church. They were married almost sixty years. Gordon was a determined man, and he wanted his own business. Finally, his determination paid off."

"In 1933 he started his own business. The business flourished, and he made his dream come true. He was always a generous man, even when he had very little to share. As his blessings increased so did his gifts to others. He financed needy families. He paid medical bills, college tuitions, gave to charities, and contributed to his church, and his giving was always discreet."

"He gave out hope and encouragement to those he met. He financed dreams with no strings attached. His life was indeed full and successful. Gordon had a loving family, a successful business, and ample wealth. His lifetime counted. He gave more to the community than he took back, and this world is a little bit better because of him."

"We hope that this nativity scene will reflect on those who pass by, who are lost and searching. May it give them hope and strength, and remind them of God's gift, Jesus Christ."

The stained glass windows designed by Lyn Hovey were given to St. James's Church in 1988 by the Harnum family in memory of Gordon Harnum.

CHAPTER 104

THE PEACE CORPS

1988
GLADYS

Louise encouraged Fred to take the early retirement package offered by IBM. Fred was only fifty-eight at the time.

"Mom, it's a fantastic package. You know Fred and I have been very frugal in our lifetime and now we can afford to do the things we never would have dreamed possible."

"But you've already traveled all over the world, Louise. What else could you possibly want to do?"

"The Peace Corps. I've always wanted to go into the Peace Corps."

"Well, how does Fred feel about that?"

"He's game to do something. I'm still trying to convince him on the Peace Corps."

"I'd hate for you to be too far away."

"Wherever we go, Mom, it will only be a plane flight away."

A week later I returned from grocery shopping to find Fred sitting at my kitchen table. He called me Mom, and told me about Louise's plan to go into the Peace Corps.

"Mom, Louise and I went to the Peace Corps office today. She asked what volunteer options were available. The representative said Africa would be a good choice. I am not looking forward to Africa but you know Louise, she is so strong-willed."

"Fred, she's always been that way, but she is smart and talented and has a lot to offer people in need."

"Right. The representative asked Louise why she wanted to join the Peace Corps, and she told him she wanted to give back to help others. He asked me the same question. Well, I'm not even sure I want to join the Peace Corps but I didn't tell him that."

"I love my wife and if she wants to go into the Peace Corps, then I want to go with her and offer my support."

As it turned out there was a coup in Africa. Their trip had to be delayed until it was safe to go. I was relieved, to be honest. Louise always loved an adventure but honestly, Africa?

While they waited for an assignment they decided to buy a camper and drive to Alaska.

I told him that was a much better plan. The thoughts of them in Africa with all the troubles and disease downright scared me.

They drove their new Toyota RV over the worst roads imaginable with miles and miles of nothing, until they finally reached Alaska. They blew twelve tires on the rocky rutted roads driving through Canada to Alaska. Before they were able to return, the assignment in Africa opened up, but they were still traveling on the road and camping. Thank goodness, they had to decline the African assignment. They took a posting in Jamaica instead.

I watched and shook my head as Louise crammed another blouse in her knapsack.

"Mom, we're only allowed one Army knapsack to hold all our belongings for a two-year assignment."

It seemed madness to me. But off they went on their Peace Corps adventure. Louise sent descriptive letters of the lifestyle and the poverty they encountered. We read all about the local foods and habits and beliefs of the Jamaicans. Fred and Louise were the only white people in the village they were assigned to.

They assisted in a boys' orphanage overseen by a Catholic priest. Louise taught the boys basic education and Fred showed them how to use a computer. Some of the boys were not orphans at all, but had been left behind so their mothers could go off the island to find work.

They rented a tiny apartment in a Jamaican household, complete with giant cockroaches. They ate chicken foot soup with rice and peas, a typical Jamaican staple that was usually rice and kidney beans. Once a week they looked forward to a bus trip to Kingston to visit the capital. They were loaded onto a colorful bus and crammed nose to nose with the locals carrying their chickens upside down to market. In Kingston, they would line up for hours at the post office or at the one telephone booth to call home. Their special treat was a real meal at McDonald's.

I was relieved when their two years of service ended. The crime rate was high in Jamaica and I always worried for their safety. On one occasion, a robber approached Louise and tried to grab her purse. Reacting quickly, she whacked the robber over his head with her umbrella and he ran away. In Jamaica a sun umbrella can make a good weapon!

CHAPTER 105

TRIP TO NEWFOUNDLAND 1989

1989
GLADYS

My home was a revolving door, and today was no different. My daughter Dot walked in, she was back from Florida for a visit. She had stopped by the house to discuss our trip to Twillingate. The doorbell rang again. It was my grandson Danny.

"Danny! What a nice surprise."

"Hi Nana, I just thought I would stop by and say hello. Hi Aunt Dot, it's great to see you too."

"Come in and sit down, we were just about to have lunch. Would you like something to eat?"

"Eat, I can always eat!" laughed Danny. Danny always had an uncanny instinct to show up just when food was about to be served.

"Ma, what do you think? Danny would like to go on the trip with us this year. Wouldn't you like your grandson to see Newfoundland?"

"He's more afraid of flying than I am, but if he wants to go, he can help with the driving. You won't mind the long drive to Twillingate, right, Dan?"

"Definitely! I'm excited. Can you pass the biscuits, please?"

"I'll buy your ticket, Danny. You're the only one of Jim's kids who has an interest in going. I think you will have great fun."

"See, he's always loved his aunt Dot. We get along well and we make each other laugh. He's a good kid."

We survived the flight to Newfoundland and picked up a rental car. Our first stop, Gordon's birthplace, Heart's Delight.

As usual, Mary and Gordon Perry had opened our home for us and put on a little heat to take out the chill. We rounded the bay at Heart's Delight and out in the distance majestic white icebergs floated by. It was such a beautiful sight, and although I grew up with them, it could still take my breath away.

"Wow, look at that! I've never seen an iceberg before." Danny perked up at the sight.

We bought some staples on the way, so we wouldn't get caught short if we had a case of the munchies. I knew how hungry boys get. We were only staying for three weeks this time and I really wanted to see my home again. We drove over to Mary and Gordon's and introduced Danny to some of his cousins.

Gordon and Mary's daughter Darlene dropped by to see us. She had a girlfriend with her and they were on their way to the Salmon Festival in St. John's to see a concert. Darlene had thick, bright, copper-red hair and was the image of her mother. They had an extra ticket and invited Danny to go with them.

He was thrilled. "I've never been to a concert. Thanks, that's great!"

"Take a jacket. It gets chilly at night in Newfoundland!" I warned. Dot reminded them all to stay out of trouble. Then they were off. It's a Rod Stewart concert, whoever he is.

I called Hilda after we'd settled in. I wanted to schedule a visit for the following week. Pete was retired and they would both be home to greet us. As we drove across the new bridge over the bay and into Twillingate, I felt joy but a profound sadness too.

I thought, I won't be back here again. I don't know why, but it just came into my head.

Hilda and Pete were a welcome sight. I had told Danny that his father visited here as a toddler. Hilda invited us in and took us right into the kitchen.

"So this is Jim's boy!" Pete and Danny shook hands. "Nice looking fella. I'll bet you're hungry too?"

"Yes, I could eat a horse if you're offering." We all laughed.

Dot looked at me and winked. I knew what she was thinking. Hey Aunt Hilda we're hungry too, but of course she fed us too. After lunch we walked past the garden that my father and grandfather had so carefully planted. Jack and Florence, Hilda and Pete's son and daughter-in-law, lived right next door in what used to be my parents' home.

Florence is a love, and Pete's son Jack still quite the character. Outspoken about Canada, he still hangs the Canadian flag upside down. Jack's a seaman like his father. Big fishing boats, and all his boys are fishermen too.

I was looking forward to seeing my old home. The house looked completely different from when I grew up in it. Jack and Florence had done a wonderful job of updating it. It just didn't look anything like what I remembered when my parents were alive, and somehow I felt sad, and a little disappointed. I had hoped to find a bit of my childhood within those four walls.

Danny brought a tape recorder and we sat with everyone while he taped all the old news and past stories. He met so many cousins, he couldn't keep track of their names.

There were second and third cousins. I was glad that Danny had the opportunity to know his roots. It was a nice trip all and all, and as always, too short. Soon we would be heading back to the states. We took one last walk around the village. I would keep those images imprinted in my mind.

CHAPTER 106

PRISCILLA & ED

1989
GLADYS

Gordon and I never thought Priscilla would re-marry. He often said to me she would never get married, and he thought that was a good thing. He didn't want her to make the same mistake and be unhappy again. After Larry died, Priscilla raised the girls on her own, maintained a career, and was financially independent. She designed and built a lovely home, and she had a small mortgage. She didn't have to marry unless it was going to make her life better.

Then Ed Denehy came along, with his charming ways and smooth talk. I suppose after seventeen years she felt tired of being single. Gordon met Ed the year before he died. We all thought he was a gentleman, and he did seem charming and well spoken. But he fooled us all.

Priscilla had arranged a small wedding for May 21, the day before her birthday. They were married at Church of the Good Shepherd in Acton. It was a small and simple wedding. Priscilla looked beautiful, with her blonde tresses and linen gown.

Ann had driven me to Priscilla's home, a mile from the church, just before the service. Either Ann wasn't paying attention or the young driver who hit us wasn't. It wasn't a major accident, just a fender bender but it gave me such a shock. I tried to act as if nothing was wrong, but I found that even in the reception line I felt reserved and preoccupied. It was the beginning sign of changes in my strength.

If Gordon had lived longer I think he would have tried to discourage Priscilla from marrying Ed. The charming husband was all an act. It soon became apparent that Ed was very controlling and manipulative. I saw an angry side of him too, and I feared for her safety.

1990s

CHAPTER 107

TRIP TO NEWFOUNDLAND 1991

1991
GLADYS

"When do you want to go to Newfoundland, Ma?" Dot asked.

"Well, I like August. It's a good time for berry picking."

"Okay, pick a date and I'll fly up with you. Tom is fine on his own. He can take care of himself in Florida and he's probably happy for me to go. Debbie will be there for him if he needs anything."

"Okay, Ma. I'll look for flights and get back to you. You know how I hate to fly but for you, Ma, I'll fly." She hugged me close.

We flew up to Newfoundland and spent the month of August visiting with Rose and Bill Bishop, playing cards and having dinner parties. We stopped in to see Mary and Gordon Perry and their family. The weather felt cool. I was glad that I had packed some warm clothes. I left my matching outfits and accessories back home and swapped them for comfortable slacks and wooly jumpers. There was a damp cold from being near the ocean, one that could chill you to the bone. However, the view out the picture window overlooked Trinity Bay and that was well worth the chill.

I loved playing Bingo and once a week we played at the Grange or the church next door to us. It gave us an evening out. It was a good thing Dot loved Bingo as much as I did. We were lucky. We won quite a bit of money.

One evening at Bingo I overheard one of the local ladies whisper to her partner that it just wasn't right that those rich ladies from the states won so often. I mentioned it to Dot and she told me to ignore them.

"Ma, forget it. They have as much chance to win as we do." She spoke out a little too loudly and I think they heard her.

I didn't go to Twillingate this time but my sister Hilda and her daughter Elizabeth came over to visit for an afternoon. It was about a four and a half hour drive from Heart's Delight to Twillingate, a long drive for me. Dot promised she would drive again next year. We had such a nice visit we decided to come back again the following summer.

CHAPTER 108

TRIP TO NEWFOUNDLAND 1992

1992
GLADYS

I knew this would be my last trip back home and Dot agreed to go with me. The fact was that I couldn't have gone without her. She always enjoyed it there too. Uldine had been up a couple of times with her husband and another time with her oldest daughter Kathy and family. Louise and Fred had been several times. Priscilla brought her girls when we went a few years back. Gordon and Bill had been there too.

One time G.H. Harnum did a trucking job on the island. My husband was so proud to have his trucks on Newfoundland soil. It meant a lot to him.

Over the years my voice had been getting weaker and weaker. The doctor suggested a speech therapist. I had always been chatty and friendly but I noticed people had difficulty hearing me. I had to be careful when I ate and drank, as sometimes I would choke. It scared me.

Dot and I were at Bingo one night when the lady beside Dot asked if I couldn't speak. It was true I didn't speak much that night, but I was perfectly able to hear her question. Dot quickly explained that I was fine and just had a very low voice. It saddened me. I felt that people were looking at me as if I was disabled or getting senile. Dot said don't pay any attention, but it took all the pleasure out of the game and I didn't want to go to Bingo after that.

Dot went to the fish market almost every day. The catch of the day was mostly cod. One day I told Dot I was in the mood for salmon. There was a hatchery nearby and she went there and got a nice piece of fresh salmon.

Sometimes she would go with her cousins, and bring a long fishing pole and catch the salmon. It was my favorite and she had them cleaned and filleted. I ate carefully as not to choke on a stray fish bone.

Near the end of our visit we went to Rose and Bill's for supper one night and I thought I might choke to death right then and there. I took a bite of a crumbly biscuit and I started choking. They slapped my back until I could clear my throat. It was frightening and I thought my time had come. After that I started writing notes and eventually I spoke less and less.

CHAPTER 109

85TH BIRTHDAY

November 1992
LOUISE

"What would you like to do for your 85th birthday, Mom?"

"Lou, I want a big family party, and I'll pay for it. Can't take it with me, right?"

"Party it is, Ma!"

I was just like my mother; I loved organizing and was great at putting a good party on.

"I want invitations sent to all the family and all my friends, maybe a hundred guests. Let's do dinner at a nice restaurant too. I don't care if it costs five thousand dollars!"

She croaked a little as she spoke, and I noticed she barely had much strength to raise her voice now, a result of the advancing Parkinson's.

"Who knows when I won't be able to speak at all? So I plan on enjoying myself as much as possible at this party!"

"Mom, it's almost December, I better get the girls to help set this in motion."

After some research and driving around, my sisters and I found the perfect place. The Sheraton Rolling Green in Lexington was convenient and an upscale hotel.

"Mom, would you like to drive over and look at their banquet room?"

"Great idea, Louise! I need to get out of this house. A nice drive would suit me just fine."

I helped her as she put on her warm overcoat, gloves, and galoshes. The weather had been icy and then had warmed up so the pavement was slippery. We drove over to Lexington and had a look at the banquet room. It was just right, and we reserved it quickly before it was booked. I ordered the invitations and we planned to hand address them, but first we would need a head count for the dinner.

Mom studied the menu closely, and she chose roast turkey, mashed potatoes, and green vegetables with brown giblet gravy. We ordered salads and a cake of course. Frannie, bless her, offered to bake a cake. We told her it would need to serve about one hundred guests.

January 1993
GLADYS

Ann took me shopping for a fancy dress today at Yolanda's, a renowned formal dress shop. I picked out a lovely raspberry chiffon dress with some beadwork on the bodice. I was pleased, and it fit me like a glove. I still had a pretty good figure for almost eighty-five. I prided myself on that. I decided on a different party color instead of my usual blue.

The party was set for Saturday January 23rd, which is the actual day I was born. However the birth record did not get filed until the 28th. So, I really have two birthdays, but believe me one is enough!

The day dawned cold but the sun was bright. A brisk breeze off the Charles River made me button up my mink as we drove to the Sheraton. I walked into the ballroom at the hotel and looked across at all my family and friends and considered how blessed I was. I wished Gordon could be here by my side; he was the only missing piece.

Children, grandchildren, great-grandchildren, and friends were there to greet me. The kids had prepared skits to entertain us. Jimmy Sheridan dressed up as Tiny Tim. He walked in with a wig and a ukulele singing "Tip Toe Through the Tulips." The room was filled with laughter. Dot was next, and she was hilarious. She was dressed up as Carol Burnett the washer-woman, in a shower cap, bathrobe, and a mop, mopping the floor as she worked her way through the tables. My grand-daughter Kim entered and waved the American flag around. She wore a First World War army uniform. I was happy to see her doing so well, such a tiny thing and I can't imagine how the uniform fit as well as it did. Last but not least Al Poulin walked around the crowd with a fat cigar in his mouth. He was dressed up to look like Groucho Marx, with the heavy mustache, thick eyebrows, and a dead rubber duck in hand. It was a great evening, and we were hysterical with laughter.

I looked out over the crowd from where we sat at the head table with my children and their spouses. There were so many grandchildren and great-grandchildren seated around tables in front of us. To think Gordon and I started all this. We were just two people in love. My friends from church and even my childhood friend Laura Ballard who was in her mid-nineties were there to celebrate my birthday. Yes, I was blessed, and I silently thanked God.

CHAPTER 110

GLADYS'S FAREWELL

1995
PRISCILLA

What we thought was a stroke was a form of Parkinson's. My mom Gladys could only drink liquids or she would choke. Her voice became affected as well. She was barely audible. Someone had to be with her all the time, and she was mostly bedridden those last months. She knew she was dying. She had even picked out a dress to wear in the casket. It wasn't her best dress. She said she didn't want to "waste" her best dress.

We apprised the family of her situation and Dot called me that night.

"Priscilla, I'm flying up tomorrow. I can stay as long as you need me."

Louise and Fred came over as much as possible. Uldine came down from New Hampshire as often as she could. Gordon and Bill and occasionally, Jim came over. Anna, Jim's ex-wife lived in our parents' house. She needed a place to stay and she had a salary and she had been good company for Mom up to that point. I worked in real estate a few towns away, and I spent some of my nights there with Dot. I came by every chance I could. My mother's hair had turned white and she was so frail. It just broke my heart. She had been the best mother a child could have. She was the person I trusted the most in my life. How would I live without her?

On the morning she died, I had slept the night in my parents' room with Dot. Both Mom and Dad had chosen to sleep in my old bedroom when they were at the end of their lives. There were glass butterflies framed above the bedhead.

Mom bought them on one of our shopping trips to Jordan Marsh years before. She kept pointing to them. Her mind was fine but her speech was limited. She wrote things down on slips of paper. I believed she wanted the butterflies to guide her to heaven.

I could have slept in the other twin bed in the room that last night but I was so frightened. I thought she would die in the night. I told Dot and I slept with her instead. I don't know what I was afraid of, because I loved my mother dearly.

In the morning Louise and Fred came. I had an open house on a listing of mine.

"Go Priscilla, there is nothing more you can do here."

I told my mother I would see her in Heaven. I was crying. I left for work and Fred came shortly after to get me at my open house. She had died soon after I left.

It was a cold January day. The funeral parlor sat next to St. James's Church. Long's was where most of our family funerals were held. Mother looked beautiful in the casket. We picked her best blue dress, the one she didn't want to "waste." She looked lovely, just like she did before she was sick.

Everyone loved her, and so many came to pay their respects and support our family during our time of grief. The caregivers from Earl's group home wheeled him up in his wheel chair. He had a small bouquet in his hands. They wheeled him over to the casket. He put the flowers on her folded hands and tears fell from his eyes. He would miss her. I wondered how much he was unable to express, being locked in his disability. We all shed tears that day, we would miss her so much.

He will swallow up death in victory:
and the Lord GOD will wipe away tears
from off all faces.
ISAIAH 25:8

RECIPES FROM DOWN HOME

OUR NEWFOUNDLAND FAVORITES

FISH & BREWIS

Ingredients:
2 pounds of fresh codfish
5 cakes hard bread
1 teaspoon of salt

Directions:
Soak bread in cold water overnight. Boil fish in salted water for about ½ hour. Remove bones, skin, and fins from the fish. Flake fish into a bowl. During the last five minutes, break the hard bread into small pieces, and add flaked fish. Mix together well and serve piping hot.

CHERRY CAKE

Ingredients:
½ cup of butter
¾ cup of sugar
3 teaspoons of baking powder
3 cups of sifted flower
5 eggs, beaten
¼ teaspoon of salt
1 teaspoon lemon juice
1 pound of cherries

Directions:
Let the cherries stand in the flour for one hour. Mix in the remaining ingredients and bake at 325° degrees Fahrenheit for 1½ hours.

G.H. HARNUM, INC.

MAJOR BUSINESS ACCOMPLISHMENTS

1970s - G.H. Harnum, Inc. moved the Simplex Wire and Cable Company's undersea fiber optics cables, and later in a joint venture with Bell Labs (Lucent Technologies) to Newington, N.H.

1972 - G.H. Harnum, Inc. hauled all the steel to construct a new bridge from Portsmouth, New Hampshire to Kittery, Maine.

1975 - G.H. Harnum, Inc. removed all the brewery equipment when Carling Black Label beer closed the Natick, Massachusetts plant.

1978 - Probably the assignment dearest to Gordon Harnum's heart was when the G.H. Harnum trucks crossed the ocean to Newfoundland to deliver a turbine and equipment to a power plant.

1979 - The Three Mile Island Reactor Number 2 in Dauphin County, Pennsylvania was the most significant U.S. commercial nuclear power plant accident. G.H. Harnum, Inc. built tanks to remove the waste and transport the oversized tanks from the site. A crane was used to lift the oversized loads around corners en route with the help of police escorts.

THE MEMORY WALL

James Harnum
1859 - 1911

Sarah Jane (Wiseman) Harnum
1871 - 1913

Elizabeth Jane (Smith) Primmer
1879 - 1936

Lucy Mary (Primmer) Sweetapple
1898 - 1944

James Primmer
1870 - 1953

Frank Jenkins
1897 - 1957

Howard Walker
1927 - 1962

Fannie (Tucker) Primmer
1896 - 1966

Larry Richard Fair
1943 - 1972

Steven Wayne Hryniewich
1957 - 1974

Heber George Mifflin Primmer
1901 - 1975

Eva Mildred (Harnum) Perry
1894 - 1975

Priscilla Anne (Legge) Wiltshire
1889 - 1975

Susannah (Primmer) Jenkins
1904 - 1976

Violet (Luff) Harnum
1897 - 1977

Jordan William Harnum
1902 - 1984

Gordon Hedley Harnum
1905 - 1987

Gladys Curtis (Primmer) Harnum
1908 - 1995

Paul Douglas Harnum
1957 - 1996

Gordon Harnum Perry
1926 - 1997

Peter Troake
1908 - 1997

Michael Neal Harnum
1953 - 1998

Thomas Noonan
1930 - 1999

Gordon Lester Harnum
1934 - 1999

Hilda Besse (Primmer) Troake
1913 - 2001

Kimberly Louise Fair
1966 - 2007

THE MEMORY WALL

Kirby Gordon Harnum
1956 - 2014

Edna Louise (Harnum) Hryniewich
1932 - 2017

Essie Pearl (Mason) Harnum
1929 - 2015

Audrey Lorraine (Jenkins) Cannuli
1932 - 2018

Neil James Harnum
1928 - 2016

Uldine Cavell (Harnum) Drown
1930 - 2018

Mary Frances (Anthony) Perry
1924 - 2016

Verna Irene (Perry) Spurrell
1945 - 2018

One final note

Although there are many websites where we can research family history, there are also many mistakes in that information. Often there are wrong dates of birth or death or incorrect spellings of names in family trees, census reports, and even on headstones. Since there are many people with the same name, it can be difficult to piece together partial information from various sources or to verify the accuracy of that information. Sometimes what we find is also quite humorous.

We found a will for James Primmer which we had hoped was prepared for Gladys's grandfather. It seems that it may have been for a distant relative instead. Below is an entry in the will that captures the essence of Twillingate during the 1800s and early 1900s.

I give and devise unto my son Robert Primmer now residing at Boston USA one of my Cod-traps, that is if he [Robert] should return to Newfoundland and require it for fishing purposes. In the meantime my son James Primmer is to have the use of it if he so requires.